How to Get a Job in School Administration

A Comprehensive Blueprint to Securing

Opportunities In Educational Leadership

VONDRE' T. WHALEY

COPYRIGHT © 2022 BY VONDRE' T. WHALEY

All rights reserved. No part of this original work may be reproduced without express written permission of the author.

Printed by:
Vondre' T. Whaley

FutureAdministrators.com

Department Leaders, LLC.

Printed in the United States of America
ISBN: 9798379379704

Independently published.

Table of Contents

How to Get a Job in School Administration

Are You Really Ready for the World of School Administration?..............1
Connect With Your Five Career Influencers 11
How to Create Your Five year Plan 22
Use Original Magnetic Content to Stand Out in a Crowded Field 38
How To Create Your 60 Second Commercial...45
How To Meet Opportunity Gatekeepers..52
Building Better Relationships with Your 5 Career Influencers..............62
Standout With Your Cover Letter, Resume, and References 69
Strategies to Get Opportunities in School Administration 85
How to Have a Great Interview...91
Popular Assistant Principal Interview Questions 97
How to Start an Academic Assistance Program...................................113
Tips for Educators Looking for a Job in School Administration.........127
Resources...132

About the Author

Vondre' T. Whaley is a native of Orangeburg, South Carolina where he graduated from Orangeburg Wilkinson High School in 1991. He attended South Carolina State University and graduated in 1995 with a degree in Biology Education and a minor in chemistry.

After 7 years of teaching physical science and physics at Orangeburg Wilkinson, he headed to Richland One as a Mission Commander at the Challenger Learning Center. While at the Challenger Center, he was instrumental in developing programming, lessons, and initiatives centered on science, technology, engineering, and mathematics. He wrote grants for the Junior Astronauts and SEMAA programs, which brought the first Aerospace Education Laboratory to the district.

He worked on the administration team as Dean of Students and Assistant Principal at A.C. Flora High School for 5 years after receiving a master's in educational administration from Grand Canyon University. Most recently, he worked as an assistant principal at Eau Claire High School, where he led the Freshman Academy team, attendance, Shamrock Watch Initiative, special education department, and the Edgenuity program.

Currently, he serves as the principal of W.J. Keenan High School, where the entire team coined the phrase, "Intentional Bonding," to focus on building relationships with young people.

While at W.J. Keenan High School, he and his team moved the school from a graduation rate of 69% to 92.3%. Also, they took the school from a state rating of below average to average within a 3-year period.

Outside of school, he has presented on state and national levels, in addition to training many teachers, department leaders, and school level administrators. He has also started a software company and is the founder and chief visionary of the Department Leaders Network, a professional learning community for K-12 department leaders.

Vondre' enjoys mentoring educators, who want to serve as school leaders and help young people go out and change the world.

He is married to Andreaetta J. Whaley, and they have two beautiful children, Vone' and Vondre' II.

You can find out more about Vondre' at https://VondreWhaley.com

You can find out more about us and the services we offer educators looking to serve as school administrators a https://FutureAdministrators.com

AUTHOR NAME

Vondre' T. Whaley

SECTION ONE

Are You Really Ready for the World of School Administration?

Serving students as a teacher or counselor takes a minimum of four years of college, a practicum, and a state certification. As you reflect on what you learned in college and what it's like working in a school system, there is no comparison. The two are totally different. The only way to truly learn how to thrive as a teacher is through real life experiences and working directly with young people.

Just like teaching, serving students as an administrator is nothing like what you think it is. It's the greatest challenge you'll ever face in the field of education, but very rewarding if your heart is in the right place.

If you desire to serve a greater number of students as a school administrator, I must ask you the following questions.

Hopefully, you'll consider your answers before moving forward in this process. Here we go.

Do you really understand what it takes?

Before we get into the nuts and bolts of this resource, which will ultimately change your life and give you a blueprint to getting an opportunity, I need you to think about this question.

Do you really understand what it takes to be an educational administrator?

It's a very tough question to answer because we are talking about servicing children, our most precious commodity.

If you are reading this, I am assuming you fall into one of the following categories.

You already have a degree in Educational Administration or you're working towards a degree in school leadership.

That means you have completed coursework or you're working towards completing a degree program where you are getting a certification, which will allow you to acquire a job in administration. But here's what's critically important for you to understand. Having a degree doesn't mean you'll be a good administrator or deserve to get a job in a supervisory role in education.

Many people have the certification and general requirements to apply for a position. However, they don't possess the intangibles or focus necessary to be considered.

Do you understand the time requirements?

As an educational administrator, you need to truly understand your time is no longer a simple routine. You can't just say, well, "at 4:30 p.m. every day I'm going home." You can't say, well, "every day at 12 p.m., I'm going to take a lunch break." Sure, you can manage your time more efficiently, but you need to be clear. Administrators make anywhere from 100 to 1,000 decisions a day. Some of those decisions involve students, teachers, parents, and community members. To work through these issues requires time and there is no set schedule. You need to have flexibility and understand it's a twenty-four-hour responsibility.

Do you really like kids?

I really need you to answer this question. Do you really like children? Good administrators need to have a genuine interest in young people. I say this all the time. You must truly believe in the kids you are working with because one day, they will change the world. And if you believe that, students will be impacted in a powerful way and believe they can be difference makers in this world. They'll go out and they'll do some amazing things. But you must truly believe in young people.

Hopefully, you're not just looking for a job in administration just to get out of the classroom or just to make a little more money. If those are your intentions, you're not going to make it. Decision makers who are hiring can see right through that. They'll know you don't love kids. So, if you like children, you're in the right place and we're going to set you up with some strategies where you will be a school administrator.

Here is a story about a teacher I once worked with. She was very smart. She knew her content area. But when she was in her classroom, she had a look of displeasure on her face. She was always frowning. You could see right through her as she was teaching her lessons. She had no patience for her students. She had no empathy for the kids, and no one wanted to be in her class.

The funny thing about this teacher is that she wanted to be a school administrator. Now, let me ask you a question. Is that the type of person you would have to be your next assistant principal, or your next principal? Is that the type of person that you want to make decisions for young people?

So, what I'm trying to say, is that you need to love kids. If you want to make a difference. If you want to have a positive effect on an entire school, you need to have a heart for the kids. That's not something you can be taught. That's not something you can learn. You must truly have an interest in kids being successful and having a part in their success.

How do you think?

Are you a one-dimensional thinker? Or do you have the capacity to think outside the box? Can you look at the bigger picture?

It's difficult for teachers, who work in a classroom for most of the day to understand things from a broader perspective. Can you think beyond those four walls? There are a lot of moving pieces to manage as a school administrator and you really need to consider the bigger picture to make things happen. You must add value on an administrative team. No one wants to have a person on their team who does not have a voice.

It's important to think about the big picture, and you have to be able to visualize situations outside the box. On average, teachers usually think about a week or a month ahead. Administrators need to have the thought capacity to think six months to a year ahead.

That's the type of thinking that you need as a school administrator. It's beyond the lesson plan. You'll need to consider how initiatives will affect the academic growth and well-being of students in the long term?

Do you have all the answers?

Let me tell you something, and this is serious. No one wants to work with a know it all. If you refuse to listen and no one can share a different opinion, you will be counterproductive on a leadership team. Successful school administrators want to work with people who have some type of value, something that will add to the team to successfully move students.

To successfully contribute to a leadership team, you must have an open mind. Many things will require trial and error. You may try one thing, and if that's not working based on data, you're going to have to turn around and try something else. So, you're going to need flexibility. You're going to have to be able to bend and that a great characteristic of an administrator.

Can you follow the vision?

Can you process and follow the vision of others? Are you able to implement strategies and initiatives to support what your supervisor or principal wants to realize in the school? Are you capable of authentically listening?

You need to have focus and follow steps to accomplish positive results. Leaders of a school never stop trying to excel, improve in academics, and building a supportive environment for students.

If you're the type of person that can't be creative, and draw people into someone else's vision, it will be difficult as an administrator. Remember, no one has all the answers. It's a collective process and you must understand that it's going to require you to work through a series of steps to realize the vision of your principal.

Are people following you?

Do you have the charisma where people are following your lead? Let's break that down a bit. First, if you're a teacher in the classroom, do your students follow you? Are your students drawn to you enough to work very hard for you? If you're a teacher in the classroom, do your co-workers follow you? Are they drawn to you? Do they see you as a teacher leader?

That's the type of charisma you're going need as a school administrator.

Let's think about this.

How do administrators within your building feel about you? Do they see you as a leader? Are you the person they consider when they need to get things accomplished?

No one is going to follow you if you're not a leader. This has nothing to do with your current position. You should be leading where you are.

Are you on time?

Are you punctual or are you one of those individuals who is always running late? Do you often have an excuse for not being in place at the time you're supposed to be there? If you're not on time, how can you be a great administrator? No one wants to follow someone who's late. If you're always running behind, people will associate that as a bad characteristic. This may ultimately cause you to lose out on valuable opportunities in leadership.

If you require people to operate in a certain manner, you must be the example. A big part of modeling what you expect requires you to be on time.

Do you know your content?

If your area is English, do you really have a great foundation in reading and writing? If your area is science, do you really have great scientific concepts where you can literally go out and teach it to the masses? If you know your content, that'll be an asset on your administrative team. If you can't walk into a classroom and evaluate what a teacher in your content area is doing, you are in trouble. It's important to have a great foundation in your area of specialty.

Can you have hard conversations?

Are you willing to have hard conversations? School administrators have difficult discussions with students, parents, teachers, and other administrators.

You can't shy away from these interactions if you desire to be a great administrator.

Do you think like an administrator?

Do you find yourself thinking, if I was in charge, I would do it this way? Do you find yourself saying, hey, this would be a great idea to accomplish this goal?

If you are constantly thinking of ways your school can improve across the board, you are already an administrator. You just don't have the position yet. You are an administrator that's currently in a teacher or counselor position.

Don't worry because you're on the right track. Decision makers are looking for people just like you to serve as school administrators.

Here is your first assignment.

Select five career influencers.

A career influencer is someone who can have a positive impact on you getting a job.

This person could be a current administrator in your building, or another school, or district. This could be a person who is retired with many connections. This could be a teacher leader who has some level of influence on other administrators or people who are making hiring decisions.

Here's one thing that you need to know. If you are applying all over the place for administrative positions, submitting your resume, sending emails, and waiting for someone to give you a call, don't be surprised if you get few responses.

In this competitive field, you are going to need people in your inner circle to guide, coach, and assist you. They are the key to your next opportunity to serve as a school administrator.

Take some time and seriously think about your five career influencers.

Action Items

✓ Make sure to sign up for our weekly newsletter at https://FutureAdministrators.com

✓ Attend one of our Future Admin Live events and consider joining our community at https://FutureAdministrators.com/live/

✓ What is the toughest question for you to answer in section one?

_____
_____

✓ How committed are you to becoming a school administrator?
(Circle one with 10 as the highest.)

1   2   3   4   5   6   7   8   9   10

✓ **Who are your five career influencers?**

_____
_____
_____
_____
_____

SECTION TWO

Connect With Your Five Career Influencers

Your assignment in section one was to choose five career influencers. Hopefully, you considered your personal network and selected individuals who have a sphere of influence that can benefit your future work opportunities.

Here's the most important thing you need to know about your five career influencers. They are your hiring team. They have the impact and the influence required to open doors leading to a school administrator position. Everyone on your list should have your respect and you can see them in a mentor role to give you guidance.

All you need to do is make the connection and let them know of your interest in becoming a school administrator.

Most people will never cross this bridge. They will not take the time to meet with a career influencer to express their intentions.

It could be fear, laziness, or simply not believing in the importance of building strong professional networks.

That's what you need to get out of your mind. You must take the necessary steps to meet with the educators on your list.

If not, you may lose out on many opportunities. You must be proactive and pick up the phone to schedule a short meeting with your career influencers.

Don't fall into this situation!

The education community is a very small circle. I've spent years building relationships with people who trust me. I also trust them and will give my honest opinion when making a recommendation for an administrative candidate.

People come to me all the time, asking if I would give them a favorable reference.

If I haven't established a real relationship with a person, I am not going to damage my trusted relationships with others in education, by giving a reference without any personal knowledge. I must truly believe the person will do a great job as an administrator. That's key.

Don't ask for references from people who barely know you and what you are capable of.

Understand basic stuff about people!

People love telling their stories. I want you to think about this. If you had the opportunity to share your story on how you became a teacher, or how you became a counselor, would you be interested? Would you be interested in sharing your story and having people listen? It's a natural human tendency to want to share things about yourself.

People also love knowing they are helping others. People want to help people. If you give people an opportunity to help you, then they will receive it. They will oblige and work very hard to see you improve, get better, and make it to the next level. Again, this is a natural human tendency.

How many people have you helped throughout your career? More than likely, you have assisted quite a few individuals. Good people love to help others. The next thing you need to understand is that people love to help people who listen.

Here's an example.

Mr. Rogers, a 28-year veteran administrator who serves as principal, is mentoring Jacob. On Monday he gave Jacob a book to read to help him get a better understanding of what it takes to be an assistant principal. When they met on the following Monday, Jacob had highlighted through the book, wrote notes in the margins, and was prepared for a meaningful discussion.

Mentors or career influencers become highly invested in your success when you follow instructions.

Ultimately, people love to know that they have impacted the lives of others.

You only need 5.

You don't need more than five career influences.

Your objective is to intentionally bond with these mentors and build strong long-lasting relationships that will be beneficial to your professional network.

You're going to have constant communication with them on a consistent basis and five is as much as you can handle.

It's like how commercials work. If you see a commercial seven or more times, you'll remember what's in the commercial and take a specific action.

I have a weakness for pizza. I see pizza commercials all the time repeatedly. I see that crust and cheese pulling up off that slice and oftentimes, I'll get on the phone. I'll make a call to order some pizza.

You're going to have the same type of relationship with your career influencers. As you contact these individuals on a consistent basis, they're going to keep you in mind when opportunities become available.

So, it's important to choose five career influences and not more than five because you'll be focusing on constant communication with them.

Here are your action steps to contacting your chosen five career influencers.

Let's talk about how to contact your career influencers.

<u>Contact each potential career influencer by phone or email to set up a meeting.</u>

This meeting should last no more than 10 minutes because you want to be considerate of another individual's time.

Here is an example of how your conversation or email should be conveyed.

"Hello (Career Influencer's Name),

I need some help with my career and think you're the person who can give me some assistance. I will respect your time and want to know if you are able to assist me. It will only take 10 minutes. When we have a specified time, we can either meet in person, through zoom, or on the telephone.

Can we schedule a day and time?

Thank you."

Is it that simple?

You will make a call or send an email with a similar message and wait for a response. If you get a favorable answer, set up a meeting and make sure you limit the meeting to 10 minutes.

You want your first interaction to be a short introduction, with a goal of expressing the following three points.

- Your commitment to advancing in your career.
- Your admiration of the career influencer's career and how they have positively impacted you.
- Get them to agree to review your plans for the future.

How to handle your 10-minute meetings.

When you get ready to meet with your career influencer, your conversation needs to go a little like this.

You're going to open it up with what I call an impact statement.

An impact statement is a comment that expresses how the person you are talking to has made a positive difference in your life or career.

Here is an example.

"First, I want you to know your work in education, and what you've done to help young people has truly made an impact on me.

I've been observing you for a while and wanted to know if you would share your educational journey with me so I can take some notes."

All you need to do is listen and take notes.

Your future mentor is going to be flattered by an opportunity to share their story. Remember, people love talking about their life experiences and goals. They are going to tell you everything about how they got into education, how they got into administration, the things they've done to help students, the things they've done to help teachers, and the things they've done to help other administrators. All you need to do at this point is LISTEN.

Next, you need to share your goal statement.

A goal statement is a comment that expresses your plans for the future backed by an action that illustrates your commitment to accomplishing your objective.

After you have listened to your career influencer's story, you need to communicate what I call a goal statement. It is also referred to as an action statement.

Here is an example.

"I am currently working on a five-year plan. My goal is to become a school administrator within this time because I want to have a greater impact on young people just like you. Are there any tips that you can give me at this time that will help me complete this five-year plan?"

Listen and take notes with any suggestions or responses they may have for your five-year plan. They may say several things such as, find a mentor at your current school, take this class, or start working with an assistant principal doing your planning to get experience. Write down everything.

Say thank you when they are done and respond something like this.

"Oh, and by the way, do you mind if I send you my five-year plan when I'm done for your review?"

In most cases, they're going to say, yes.

This is your opportunity to show them that you are a person who is proactive. Remember, people love helping people who help themselves. People love helping people who are action takers.

At the end of your ten-minute conversation, the following things will be achieved.

You've listened to your career influencer.

You've asked your career influencer for help.

You've taken notes.

You've shown your career influences gratitude.

You've made a commitment to follow up and send them your five-year plan which proves to them you are serious.

Now, I would like to share a few of my career influencers with you.

Dr. Joan Kozlovsky

Dr. Kozlovsky is a former superintendent and consultant. I first met her when I was working at a high school as Dean of Students, and she served as a consultant. I took a liking to Dr. Kozlovsky because she was very personable, and she has had a long career in education impacting thousands of people. During a conversation, I shared with her that I wanted to learn everything that she had to offer. One of my goals was to become an assistant principal and one day leading and moving an entire school. She took that to heart, which had led to many conversations on a consistent basis. When I was ready to go into administration, she set up meetings for me with people within her sphere of influence. These meetings led to me getting an opportunity in administration. She is still one of my mentors to this day and our relationship has lasted over 15 years and counting. She is like family to me.

Dr. Jake Sello

Dr. Sello has served as a teacher, assistant principal, principal, area superintendent, and superintendent. I first met him during an interview, where I shook everyone's hand and introduced myself before answering questions for a job with a special science and engineering program. Dr. Sello was impressed by my energy and compassion for serving young people and has been mentoring me ever since.

We have had meetings where he shares books, articles, and scenarios. He listens and allows me to give feedback, which has helped my professional growth.

When I was searching for opportunities in administration, he didn't hesitate to make phone calls to introduce me to decision makers who wanted to hire people with strong leadership skills.

As principal, Dr. Sello continues to be a valuable mentor and dear friend.

Mr. Richard McClure

Mr. Richard McClure is a former principal, who mentored me as a young administrator, and taught me how to be a principal. As his dean of students and assistant principal, he had me involved in every decision-making situation. He also allowed me to independently lead initiatives where I was able to learn from mistakes and get incredible feedback through many one-on-one conversations.

When I started as principal, it was a very seamless transition.

I told him I wanted to soak up everything like a sponge to one day lead a school, and he took my comments very seriously. To this day, I am extremely grateful to have learned from such a great school administrator who cared about all children.

Here is your second assignment.

Contact your five career influencers using the framework described in this section.

School Administrators are action takers. This is a very short lesson, but it is crucial. Think of your five career influencers as your hiring team. Make the phone calls, schedule the meetings, take the notes, and use the information to develop your 5-year plan, which we will talk about in section 3.

Action Items

✓ Make sure to sign up for our weekly newsletter at https://FutureAdministrators.com

✓ Attend one of our Future Admin Live events and consider joining our community at https://FutureAdministrators.com/live/

✓ How comfortable are you with contacting your career influencers?
(Circle one with 10 as the highest.)

1 2 3 4 5 6 7 8 9 10

✓ **List 3 goals you would like to accomplish in the next year.** (You may want to include this information in your 5-year plan)

_____
_____
_____
_____
_____
_____

SECTION THREE

How to Create Your Five-Year Plan

In this section, we will be discussing how you can put together your five-year plan, but first, I want to point out the importance of not following the crowd.

If you ask most people what their plan is, 9 times out of 10, they will respond, there is no plan. Most times they follow the crowd. You know, this reminds me of a recent phenomenon on Facebook. Facebook started their avatar program, where members could create their own little cartoon like image of themselves. At one point, almost everyone had an avatar loaded to their profile for the world to see.

Here's what I did to stand out.

I created my own avatar. I painted a picture of myself and that became my avatar on Facebook. It's a lot different than the Facebook avatar. So many, many people wanted to know how they could get an avatar like the one I developed. My response was very direct.

First, you need to get a canvas.

Next, you need to get some paintbrushes and paint.

Finally, you need to draw and paint a picture of yourself.

Here's the problem. For most people, to come up with a unique caricature as described requires work, and they're not willing to do it.

If you stand out, do something different, and put in the work, you will be seen. You will get the opportunities. My avatar became so popular, I had to put it on a t-shirt. People love my avatar. I stand out. I am different and I will get the opportunities. That's the mindset that you must have when you're looking for a job in school administration.

This section emphasizes standing out because being different will open doors. The major way for you to stand out and communicate to your five career influencers about how focused you are is to create your five-year plan.

In addition to the notes you have taken, consider the following segue positions as potential milestones or steps along your journey to include in your document.

Segue positions are job assignments outside the classroom that will lead to an opportunity in school administration.

Teacher on Special Assignment

The first segue position we are going to discuss is called a Teacher on Special Assignment, also referred to as a TOSA. The great thing about this assignment is that it allows the educator to see the school from a broader perspective. Typically, the TOSA is going to work alongside a member of the administrative team. They may work on professional development, academic initiatives, assisting with teacher observations, and student support.

TOSA's can get a better understanding of how a school operates, often meet with the administrative team, and gain valuable experiences that may lead to an administrative position.

Assistant Administrator

The next segue position we're going to discuss is called Assistant Administrator, or AA for short. In this capacity, the AA is a part of the administrative team, and they are completing duties alongside an assistant principal. If you have an assistant principal that's in charge of the graduation rate, an assistant administrator may be working on their team collecting data and meeting with students.

The AA may also have a level of discipline which gives him or her the opportunity to deal with behavioral situations with students. Assistant Administrators are allowed to make decisions and learn the daily operations of a school.

Dean of Students

The Dean of Students, also known as the DOS, works primarily with student services. This person may run student government or supervise the academic clubs at a school. The DOS usually plans all the pep rallies, field trips, or anything else dealing with Student Services. He or she may also work with discipline in conjunction with an assistant principal. Again, a great position to segue into the position of assistant principal. I had the privilege of serving as a Dean of Students, and it was an amazing experience.

Lead Teacher

Lead teachers are usually assigned work on a specific academic program, instead of teaching a full schedule. For example, a lead teacher that's over a magnet program for engineering may also focus on a specific subject. If a school needs improvement in math and teachers need additional support, a principal may choose a lead teacher to work with math.

Lead teachers get the opportunity to increase their perspective, look at school data, and participate in discussions to improve academic achievement. It's a great position for a teacher who wants to specialize in curriculum and instruction on an administrative team.

Graduation Coach

A graduation coach helps administrators manage the graduation rate at a high school. He or she may also set up college field trips, help students explore career opportunities, and work with parents to help them navigate through the process of helping their senior graduate. Graduation coaches look at every cohort from 9th to 12th grade to ensure students are on the right track to graduate. They may also have the responsibility of making sure students are college and career ready, which involves internships and high stakes testing such as the SAT, ACT, and ASVAB.

Athletic Director

The athletic director or the AD manages all the athletics at a school. This includes dealing with students who are athletes, managing an athletic tutoring program, working with coaches, and managing games. The AD is responsible for distributing tickets, managing the money and revenues that generate from athletic programs, putting together reports, and giving presentations as it relates to athletics on a campus. This experience is a great segue into an assistant principalship.

When you are writing your five-year plan, it's a great idea to include segue position as a goal.

Now, let's answer the following question.

How are you going to impact academic achievement outside the classroom?

Oftentimes, teachers believe their body of work inside the classroom speaks for itself. If they are a great classroom teacher, then they should be a great school administrator.

You need to understand administration and teaching are two separate things that are both required to operate a school.

Decision makers such as principals are looking for individuals who have made an impact outside the classroom. So, how can you make a difference in academics for the entire school beyond your current students? Here are a few strategies to consider.

Manage a Data Room

Volunteer to manage a data room. A data room is nothing more than a listing of students, along with points of data that can be used to make decisions to move the school forward. For example, you may have a room where you have pictures of every kid in your school with their attendance, behavior, and academic data. Based on certain trends, administrators may be able to see areas where improvement is required. If you are managing a data room, you are impacting academic achievement outside of the classroom, and that's one way to gain great experience while you're currently teaching.

Manage a Tutoring Program

Every school has students who need extra support with core subjects such as math, English, science, and social studies. You can manage a tutoring program. In some cases, schools pay the person to provide these services to students. Basically, you will manage the after-school tutoring program outside of school. You'll track these students, make sure they're attending on a regular basis, and look at their grades to make sure they are improving.

If there is not a tutoring program at your school, ask your administrators about volunteering to help students.

Think about this for a moment. If you were sitting at an interview table, you would be able to talk about how you have assisted students with a tutoring program. You can also discuss how those students moved from one point to a higher point, which looks great towards getting your next opportunity.

Manage an Academic Assistance Program

One of my personal favorites is to manage an Academic Assistance Program at your school. This will require you to work with at least 20 students who need academic support and support on all levels. This includes monitoring their progress, working with them after school, and communicating with their teachers and parents. As the director of the program, you'll create student success plans for all your participants.

When you have conversations with decision makers, you'll be in a position to say, "I manage this Academic Assistance Program and I took my students from where 50% of the students were failing to less than 5% at the end of the program."

The idea of this strategy is so important, therefore I am devoting a complete section in this book to setting up an Academic Assistance Program at your school. This is a great segue into an administrative position because it shows that you're taking the initiative by working with students to improve academic performance.

Manage an Engagement Library

The next thing that you can do is create what I call an Engagement Library. This is new stuff. You haven't seen this anywhere, but this is a strategy that can be used to help improve academic achievement. An engagement library is a room that has materials teachers can check out to increase classroom engagement. For example, a beach ball that can be used as a conversation ball to be thrown from one student to the next to provide feedback. The room may include whiteboards where students can make Venn diagrams. You might find balls that can be rolled, thrown, and poster paper that can be used to give feedback. All these things can be checked out by teachers.

You can be the teacher who takes the initiative to do this for your school. Manage the check-in / check-out process. This makes a great conversation at the table when interviewing for an assistant principal position.

All these ideas to increase academic achievement on a schoolwide level can be added to your five-year plan.

Here is the next question I want you to answer.

How are you using your leadership skills outside the classroom specifically for operations?

In addition to making an impact on academics schoolwide, you should also get experience or exhibit how you are using your talents to assist with operations.

Here are a few examples.

Manage your Hallway

Take leadership in managing your hall. This requires a meeting with teachers working on your hall to discuss transitions from one class to another. Ask teachers how can we improve students moving from class to class after the bell?

In addition to standing at the door between classes, it may require some other type of strategy such as holding up a red card when it's a minute left to get in class.

Ask teachers how can we improve students marked as tardy on our hallway? Again, these are conversations you can lead to manage the process. What about ideas to improve behavior on the hallway?

After every meeting, put this information in writing, submit it to all teachers on the hall, and monitor the progress.

This will allow you to say you served as the teacher leader over hallway transitions, where your responsibility was to meet with teachers, track tardiness, behavior, and collaboratively come up with ways to improve? It would be even better if you tracked everything with spreadsheets, charts, and graphs to share as a visual.

Sponsor a Club

You can sponsor a club such as the National Honor Society, Beta Club, or chess club, where you take a leadership initiative to work with students in something they are interested in outside of the classroom. Pick a club no one wants to work with. There's always a club where administrators are looking for someone to sponsor. Raise your hand and volunteer to work with that specific club. That's a great conversation piece that you can have with your career influencer or at an interview table.

Yearbook Advisor

The most challenging project at a school is creating a yearbook, especially if it is not an elective class where students meet on a regular basis. Because it requires much attention to detail, administrators often find it difficult to get someone to manage this initiative.

Although it typically comes with a stipend, you can volunteer to work with the yearbook.

You'll manage kids going out to take pictures, work with others to come up with creative ideas, and use graphics software to design pages. In some cases, it also requires managing the sales of the yearbook and distribution.

The final product is something that you can share with a career influencer and talk about doing an interview for an administrative position.

Manage Student Events

You can manage a pep rally or a program for parents at your school that requires someone to work through the details and delegate. As a matter of fact, you should volunteer to manage several programs during the year, which will make you an asset to your principal.

Every experience will allow you to learn and contribute to the success of your school.

PTSO, SIC, other organizations.

You can work with the Parent Teacher Student Organization, PTSO, or the School Improvement Council, SIC, or any organization at your school. This will require meeting with parents after school and planning various initiatives to improve school culture.

Your objective is to display your leadership skills outside the four walls of a classroom. What are you doing? You are a leader. All we need you to do is show it.

What books are you going to read?

It's important to read books in your industry because the information that you learn will help with professional growth. Educators should read at least two books per year on leadership or strategies to improve academic achievement. Here are my two personal favorites.

Teach like a Pirate by David Burgess.

This book is all about classroom engagement and strategies you can use to get young people excited about learning.

The Principal by Michael Fullan.

This book is great for individuals who want to go into the field of administration because it talks about building professional capacity within your team and how to build leaders within your school.

Your five-year plan should include industry specific books you plan to read. Make a list based on recommendations or areas you feel need improvement.

What type of professional development can you participate in?

Think about the professional development offered within your district, regionally, and nationally. You should also think about what you can take virtually all over the world. Oftentimes, all you need to do is sit down and ask your principal or building level supervisor if he or she will pay for you to attend this professional development.

Every opportunity to learn something different will better prepare you for your next opportunity to serve as a school administrator.

Here is your third assignment.

Write your five-year plan and send it to your five career influencers. You should have all the information, strategies, and tips from your five career influencers to help you develop your five-year plan. You should have also answered several questions that we have discussed in this section.

How are you going to impact academic achievement outside of the classroom? How are you going to use your leadership skills outside the classroom, specifically in operations? What books are you going to read to improve yourself as a professional educator? What types of professional development would you like to attend to improve your teaching craft, or to give you additional skills that will help you become an administrator?

You may want to become an administrator after your first or second year into your five-year plan. That's great! Where are you going to be in five years? If your goal is to become a principal, or work on a district level in some capacity, include it in your five-year plan.

When you are done, email this five-year plan to your five career influences. If you have their physical address, it will be even better if you send them a letter that includes your five-year plan.

Remember, most people will not take the time to complete this step. This is why we started this section with the advantage of being different.

Look at the example below.

Your Name Goes Here – 5 YEAR PLAN

My ultimate goal is to serve as an educational administrator in a high school to have a greater impact on students in my community. (You can edit)

Goals	YEAR ONE
Personal	• I will exercise at least 3 days per week • I will lose 15 pounds
Current Position	• I will have a student passage rate of 90% or more in all my classes • I will send at least 20 "great Job" letters to parents to recognize students who are doing well.
Professional Advancement	• I will go on a minimum of 5 job interviews to get a job as a Dean of Students or Assistant Administrator
Initiatives to Impact the Entire School	• I will manage a data room at my school • I will start an engagement room at my school
Professional Development	• I will attend a workshop on project-based learning • I will attend a training on strategies to teach virtually
Books	• I will read Teach Like A Pirate by Dave Burgess • I will read The Principal by Michael Fullan

Reward Promise:

As a reward for completing my goals for year one, I promise to go on a weekend vacation to Myrtle Beach in South Carolina.

Signature to myself: _____ Date: _____

You can find our Five-Year Plan template at https://FtureAdministrators.com/templates

It's important to complete goals for each year, which means your document should be at least five pages. This is important because you want your career influencers to know you put much thought into the document.

There are several sections of our template for you to list goals in different areas of your life. This includes personal, current position, and professional advancement. It also includes goals you want to accomplish that impact the school, professional development, and books you want to read. At the end of the year, if you accomplish all your objectives, there is an area for you to write how you are going to reward yourself.

When you are finished, sign the document, and get it out to your five career influencers.

This will do several things for you.

Your five career influencers will know you are serious.

It gives you another opportunity to reach out to your five influencers to get feedback.

You get an opportunity to establish a mentor / mentee relationship with your five career influencers.

In section four, we will discuss additional ways you can stand out ahead of your competition.

Action Items

- ✓ Make sure to sign up for our weekly newsletter at https://FutureAdministrators.com

- ✓ Attend one of our Future Admin Live events and consider joining our community at https://FutureAdministrators.com/live/

- ✓ What is the goal of your five-year plan?

_____
_____
_____
_____

- ✓ How will you make an impact outside your classroom in academics and school operations?

_____
_____
_____
_____
_____
_____

SECTION FOUR

Use Original Magnetic Content to Stand Out in a Crowded Field

If you are reading this book, you are already different. Most people will not invest in such a resource and read it. Let's review what typically happens.

An aspiring school administrator goes to school, acquires a degree in educational administration, and passes a test to get the certification. Then, they get online, start applying for jobs, and send out their resume. After a while, the aspiring school administrator quickly realizes their efforts are yielding little to no results.

There were more than 120 applicants for the last assistant principal position I filled. The competition is fierce.

The crowded field of educators looking to get into administration is why it's important to stand out.

Let's review what you should have done so far.

Number ONE. You should have made the decision to become a school administrator.

Number TWO. You should have selected your five career influencers.

Number THREE. You should have contacted those influencers, set up meetings, and conducted those meetings.

Number FOUR. You should have completed your five-year plan and sent them to your five career influencers.

Number FIVE. You need to follow your five-year plan and continue to focus on being a great teacher or counselor. Remember, your ultimate goal is to stand out amidst of a huge crowd.

How can you stand out?

One of the best ways for you to stand out is to create what I call Original Magnetic Content, otherwise known as OMC. Original Magnetic Content is short industry specific information covering the latest topics people like and share with others.

When you create OMC, it puts you in a position of authority.

It allows important decision makers in the industry to remember who you are and that's what you want to happen. You want to stand out!

Here is what you should do with your original magnetic content.

Share it with your five career influencers.

Share it with opportunity gatekeepers.

Opportunity gatekeepers are educational professionals outside of your five career influencers who can get you in front of a decision maker.

Principals, assistant principals, district personnel, secretaries with personal power, and other staff who have an influence on people who make hiring decisions, are all examples of possible opportunity gatekeepers.

You can share through e-mail, social media, or physical mail. It's about being consistent and staying at the top of peoples' mind when they are looking for a school leader.

How to create Original Magnetic Content?

Here's what I want you to remember. The magic is in the action, not in the steps. I can literally give you 10 steps to this process. However, those 10 steps may take you so long, it'll never get done.

You need to take action, so, I'll give you three.

Follow these steps every time you decide to create a new piece of content to share with others.

Step 1: Use Google to search "Top Education Trends".

The first step is to use Google, the world's most popular search engine. Go to Google and type in "Top Education Trends." That's going to give you a series of articles to use for OMC.

Make sure you browse through the articles and look for something that piques your interest and is relevant in today's educational climate.

Step 2: Select an article and make 3-5 bullet points.

Select an article and write 3 – 5 bullet points summarizing the main ideas. You want your reader to get the gist of the article after reading your OMC. Think of your content as CliffsNotes for the reader.

Step 3: Write sentences, record audio, or video for each point.

For each bullet point, create a short article by writing 3 – 5 sentences for each bullet point. You can also take out your phone and record yourself talking about each bullet point to create an audio. A third option is to make a short video by recording yourself talking about the main points of your content. If you are creative, you can produce all three forms of information.

The key is sharing short forms of content. An article can be as short as 9 to 12 sentences. An audio or video can literally be less than a minute and no more than three minutes.

Let's go over an example.

3 Ways to Teach Empathy in Your Classroom

Empathy is feeling with or sharing the same emotional reaction to a situation. Typically, if you can have empathy with others regarding an incident or period of time, you can learn and understand on a deeper level.

This is different from sympathy, which deals with having feelings for or acknowledging an emotional reaction without having a direct personal understanding.

Here are 3 ways to teach empathy in your classroom.

Allow students to brainstorm similar personal experiences they have encountered. For example, if you are teaching a story where the main character loses a close family member, ask students to remember a time when they may have lost someone that has meant a great deal to them.

Ask students to describe how the character feels from their point of view. Encourage them to put themselves in the shoes of a character and relate it to their modern day lives.

Challenge students to use their cameras to take pictures of themselves and team members showing facial expressions of a particular character in a story and write descriptions.

Taking risks in the classroom and allowing your students the flexibility of expression is highly instrumental in teaching empathy.

-End of Article-

It took less than 30 minutes to write this article and you can easily develop one piece of OMC each week.

Here is your fourth assignment.

Create three to five pieces of original magnetic content and share them using the strategies below.

What Can You Do with Your Original Magnetic Content?

-Send an email or physical letter with your OMC to your 5 career influencers.

-Send an email or physical letter with your OMC to all the opportunity gatekeepers you've met.

-Post your content on all social media platforms, including Twitter, Facebook, LinkedIn, TikTok, and Instagram.

Action Items

- ✓ Make sure to sign up for our weekly newsletter at https://FutureAdministrators.com

- ✓ Attend one of our Future Admin Live events and consider joining our community at https://FutureAdministrators.com/live/

- ✓ In addition to your 5 Career Influencers, list 5 Opportunity Gatekeepers you can send your Original Magnetic Content?

  _____
  _____
  _____
  _____
  _____

- ✓ What topics are you considering for developing Original Magnetic Content?

  _____
  _____
  _____
  _____
  _____
  _____

SECTION FIVE

How to Create Your 60 Second Commercial

Whether you realize it or not, every time you have a conversation with a potential decision maker or someone with influence in education, it's a job interview. This is why it's extremely important to be clear on your communication and know how to effectively describe your worth and skillsets. The best way to prepare yourself is to create a 60 second commercial or personal statement you can share with opportunity gatekeepers.

A personal statement or 60 second commercial is a brief description that typically highlights a person's academic or professional qualifications, personal background, and goals. It is often used in introductory conversations to share belief systems and objectives.

Personal statements are no more than one minute in length and allow the writer to express their thoughts, experiences, and goals in a clear and concise manner. They are used to give the listener or reader a sense of the person behind the message.

Personal statements can be used for a variety of purposes, but mainly as a way to introduce yourself to a potential employer or networking contact.

It's important to remember that a personal statement reflects what you believe in and what you want to accomplish, so it should be well-written, concise, and a true representation of who you are as a professional.

The Personal Statement Exercise

Complete the following statements.

I believe all children ...

_____

_____

My responsibility as an educator is ...

_____

_____

As an educator, I realize …

_____

_____

As a team player, I understand …

_____

_____

My most important goal as an educator is …

_____

_____

I expect students to …

_____

_____

For students to effectively learn, they need …

_____

_____

When you are done, look at all 7 statements and put them in order from the most important in chronological order.

Next, look at the top 2 statements and write them in a complete sentence that can be communicated in 60 seconds or less.

When you are done, you will have your very own personal statement.

Next steps after creating your 60 Second Commercial

Use Microsoft Word or any word processing software on your computer and type your 60 second commercial as large as you can on one page. Print out five copies, which will serve as posters to place in different places.

Post three posters around your house in places that you frequent often. Your refrigerator, bathroom mirror, and clothing closet are great places to have one of your posters.

Then, post two at work where you can read it on a daily basis.

Here is why you ought to do this.

You need to remember your 60 second commercial. You need to say it to your students, co-workers, administrators, and everyone you come in contact with in the field of education.

If you use your 60 second commercial often, it will manifest in your career.

Why are personal statements important?

Personal statements are memorable. If you use them on a regular basis, people will remember you and what you stand for.

The next thing to keep in mind is very few people effectively utilize a personal statement. If you use this strategy, you will stand out.

How can you use your personal statement?

Share your personal statement or 60 second commercial with your students daily. It will give you practice, and will let your students know how you feel about them and what you want to accomplish professionally.

Tell your administrators and other colleagues. Remember, it's your personal statement and when people hear it over and over again, it will stick in their minds, just like a commercial. So, you want to make sure you use your personal statement.

You should also put your personal statement in your email signature. This will give people the opportunity to read what you believe in every time you send an email.

You should also put your personal statement on all of your social media sites such as Facebook, LinkedIn, Twitter, or any other social media site you are involved with.

If you create your own letterhead or business cards, include your personal statement.

It's all about promoting your brand, which may get a decision maker to consider you if an opportunity becomes available.

Now, let me share my 60 second commercial.

"I believe young people will ultimately change the world. It's our responsibility as professional educators to provide the resources, education, and support required so they can believe it too."

If you look at my personal statement, you'll see that I combined the first two statements from our earlier exercise to develop my 60 second commercial.

I say it every single day. As a matter of fact, I say it so much, people on my team have adopted a variation of my statement as their own.

I even have students come up to me all the time and say, Mr. Whaley, I am going to change the world. That's the power of a 60 second commercial.

Here is your fifth assignment!

Redefine your personal statement. Can you shorten it up? Are there some words you need to include?

Then I want you to go ahead and print out those 5 posters. Put three in your house and two at your workplace.

Memorize it and begin to share it daily, which will help you when you have conversations with opportunity gatekeepers or your five career influencers, who can lead you to your next opportunity to serve.

Action Items

- ✓ Make sure to sign up for our weekly newsletter at https://FutureAdministrators.com

- ✓ Attend one of our Future Admin Live events and consider joining our community at https://FutureAdministrators.com/live/

- ✓ Write your 60 second commercial in the space below.

_____
_____
_____
_____
_____
_____
_____

- ✓ Where are you going to post your personal statement posters?

_____
_____
_____
_____

SECTION SIX

How to Meet Opportunity Gatekeepers

My favorite animal is the lion. They are very social creatures. Lions stand out among other animals because of their structure. They are ferocious. Lions also understand for them to survive, they must hunt. Lions are very intentional. They go where the action is.

Do you think like a lion? Are you a hunter?

If you want to get your next opportunity, you can't sit on the sidelines waiting for the coach to put you in the game. You must hunt!

In this case, to get your next job as a school administrator, you have to meet as many opportunity gatekeepers as possible.

An Opportunity Gate Keeper is either a decision maker themselves or has influence with someone who is a decision maker. (Ex. principals, assistant principals, district personnel, and secretaries who have influence on administrators)

If you know enough opportunity gatekeepers, you will increase your chances of getting a position as a school administrator. Here's what I want you to do now. Answer the following question.

How many opportunity gatekeepers would know you if your name came up in a conversation? (Write their names below.)

_____
_____
_____
_____
_____
_____

Most people can list no more than seven. If you list seven, you're doing okay, but that's not good enough. You must commit yourself to meeting as many opportunity gatekeepers as possible.

Let's talk about how to meet opportunity gatekeepers!

Your first move is to look at your own building. You have a principal, assistant principal, and maybe a few secretaries, who have great influence on decision makers.

During your planning period or after school, set up a brief meeting with these individuals. You simply want to share your interest in school leadership. You should also ask them about the best ways for you to get an opportunity as a school leader?

These meetings are like your meetings with your five career influencers, but they're not as in depth. Your goal is to share your interest in becoming an administrator. If you have one principal, and three assistant principals, you need to do your very best to have four meetings.

Next, you want to go where the action is, just like a lion. Where do opportunity gatekeepers hang out? Where can you meet opportunity gatekeepers? Let's make a quick list.

Number ONE. Opportunity gatekeepers such as principals, assistant principals, and district personnel are always at board meetings.

Number TWO. You can find opportunity gatekeepers at sporting events. More than likely, they will be the individuals who are on some type of duty, monitoring students, and guests at the event.

Number THREE. You can find opportunity gatekeepers at industry specific professional development.

Number FOUR. You can find opportunity gatekeepers at industry related organization events. Administrators and school leaders attend the same conferences and meetings.

In addition to the four places, we listed where you can meet opportunity gatekeepers, the best place to find them is in their schools.

Here are two ways to gain access.

Shadow an administrator.

You can set up shadowing days at the opportunity gatekeeper's school. Now this shadowing should take no more than 30 minutes to an hour. That will give you enough time to meet the person and get to know them on a more personal level. You also want to learn a few things as well.

Make sure you state your personal statement or your 60 second commercial during your shadowing experience.

In addition to taking notes, make sure to get contact information and a recommendation of good industry specific books to read. If you get a book title, you are giving the opportunity gatekeeper a chance to have an impact on your journey. You want this act of kindness to continue and may lead to an opportunity in the future.

Let's go over a few tips on how to set up a quick shadowing day with an opportunity gatekeeper.

<u>The first thing I want to do is call principals you are interested in shadowing.</u>

Make sure to also send an email to his or her secretary. Keep in mind, many principals have their secretary handle all their communications. So, if you send an email, make sure you copy the secretary. If you make a phone call, don't get upset if you are directed to the principal's secretary. Oftentimes, they are just as good as talking to the principal.

If you cannot get in contact with the principal, it may be easier to contact an assistant principal.

Remember, assistant principals are also opportunity gatekeepers. They have a strong influence on decision makers, especially the principal.

Give it about five days and if you don't get any responses from the principal, then try his or her assistant principal. If you get a shadowing day with an assistant principal, you may also meet the principal within that 30 minute to an hour timeframe.

Here is a simple script that you can use when contacting principals and assistant principals.

"Hello, my name is _____,

I have been observing your school for some time, and like what your team is doing from a leadership standpoint. My goal is to one day serve as a school administrator. I was wondering if you would consider allowing me to shadow you for 30 minutes to an hour, which would help me learn and grow professionally?"

You may change up the script as much as you like but keep it simple.

<u>Now here's the plan.</u>

Contact as many opportunity gatekeepers as possible with a phone call or email. Wait up to five days for a response. If you don't hear from anyone, send a second contact with the same message.

You should be able to set up several shadowing experiences using this strategy.

Set up quick 15-minute interviews!

People love to talk about themselves. You can use this fact to help you meet opportunity gatekeepers. All you need to do is ask to interview them about an education-related topic. The content from this interview can be used to create Original Magnetic Content.

These brief interviews should last no more than 15 minutes, but will give you an opportunity to learn about them a little more and share your interest in becoming a school administrator.

Plus, there is a major benefit.

You will be promoting them by sending out your OMC. This sets them up as an authority in their field.

Your interview strategy is a perfect example of the Law of Reciprocity.

The Law of Reciprocity is a social principle based on the idea that people will repay a positive action with another positive action and a negative action with another negative action. It is often used in social and business relationships to establish trust and mutual obligation. The idea is that when someone does something for us, we feel obligated to repay the favor, leading to a cycle of reciprocated actions. The principle can be seen in many aspects of human behavior, such as gift-giving, social exchange, and building and maintaining relationships.

Your interview and OMC are positive actions that will most likely result in the opportunity gatekeeper helping you find a school administrator position in return.

Here is a simple script for setting up an Original Magnetic Content interview. Remember, intentionality.

"Hello, my name is _____,

Currently, I am working on some educational content to help schools. I admire what you and your team are doing to help students and was wondering if you would grant me an interview to be featured in a story I'm working on?"

It's that simple. Change it up if you need to but keep it simple.

Here are some additional benefits of doing a 15-minute interview.

When you create the Original Magnet Content, this also gives you an opportunity to send it back to them with a thank you note or a thank you message. When they get your OMC, they're going to send it to all their friends, who are most likely opportunity gatekeepers as well.

By completing the interview and creating OMC, you are letting the opportunity gatekeeper know you are a person who follows through. This will help them remember you when administrative positions become available.

Use this smart tip when interacting with opportunity gatekeepers.

During your conversations with opportunity gatekeepers, make sure to share your 60 second commercial. It doesn't matter if it's during a shadowing experience, an interview you set up, or a sporting event. Find a way to interject your personal statement.

At the end of each conversation, make sure you say something like this.

"Oh, by the way, I really enjoyed talking with you and learning your insight on education and working with young people. I have some educational content that I've been working on. Would you mind me sending it to you so I can get your feedback?"

This gives you the opportunity to get their contact information and send them some of your Original Magnetic Content.

Every contact you make builds a stronger relationship, which increases the likelihood they will remember you when opportunities come around.

Here is your 6th assignment.

Create a calendar and list events and opportunities to meet opportunity gatekeepers.

Include the following:

Board meetings you want to attend.

Sporting events you want to attend.

Industry specific events you want to attend.

Make phone calls and send emails to set up shadowing experiences. Then, add it to your calendar.

Make phone calls and send emails to set up opportunity gatekeeper interviews. Then, add it to your calendar. Don't forget to follow through by creating and sending out OMC.

Action Items

✓ Make sure to sign up for our weekly newsletter at https://FutureAdministrators.com

✓ Attend one of our Future Admin Live events and consider joining our community at https://FutureAdministrators.com/live/

✓ List seven opportunity gatekeepers you would like to shadow.

_____
_____
_____
_____
_____
_____
_____

✓ What questions would you ask an opportunity gatekeeper during a 15-minute interview?

_____
_____
_____
_____
_____

SECTION SEVEN

Building Better Relationships with Your 5 Career Influencers

It is important to focus on building and growing your professional network, which should include your 5 career influencers. To illustrate the effectiveness of career influencers, look at what happened during the week I had a vacancy open for an assistant principal.

First Interaction

An assistant principal from another school gave me a call to suggest a young lady who he's been mentoring. He expressed how she would be great for the assistant principal position.

Second Interaction

A former principal and district level administrator gave me a call about a gentleman he has been working with. He wanted to convey how this young man would be a great fit for my team and how his contribution would help move my students forward.

Third Interaction

I received a third call from a guidance counselor and a former assistant principal. He wanted me to consider a young man for my assistant principal opening and gave me some examples of how this young man is currently working with students. As a result of the call, this reference was contacted for an interview.

Fourth Interaction

I got a final call from a retired teacher to recommend a young lady who was in her social studies department when she served as department leader. She wanted me to know her former colleague was ready to tackle the tasks of being a school administrator.

Here is what I want you to understand. All these calls I received in a week were from career influencers.

Career influencers are a powerful addition to your hiring team, and you should have five of them.

Ultimately, your goal is to build a true relationship with each one of them, which requires consistent interactions.

Don't fall into this example.

A young lady called me to set up a meeting, which lasted about 25 minutes. I gave her some strategies and we discussed her future aspirations of becoming a school administrator.

After the short meeting, I didn't hear anything else from her for the remainder of the year. Towards the end of the year, she started asking me to give her recommendations for open administrator positions.

I refused because we never established a good relationship, and I didn't get the opportunity to learn her skillsets. I couldn't match her with any decision makers in my circle of influence, who were looking to fill certain areas on their administrative teams.

This example illustrates the importance of building a solid relationship with your five career influencers.

They must know you are committed and willing to put in the work. It starts with establishing a mentor-mentee relationship.

All you have to do is have a simple conversation like the example below to establish an ongoing learning opportunity.

"I really consider you an educator, who has made an impact on my professional career. Can we meet or have a conversation on the phone at least once per month? I would love to update you on my progress and get feedback as I travel along my educational journey."

When your career influencer says yes, you must be consistent with initiating every interaction.

Here is how this strategy works!

You are going to have to set up a calendar because you have 5-career influencers. Your calendar should be spaced out where you will have at least one meeting each week with a different mentor. Because you have five, one week should consist of two meetings.

3 benefits of this strategy

It's going to keep you focused on your ultimate goal, which is to become a school administrator.

Every week, you will be working toward your goal, and learning valuable lessons from people who are well connected in the education industry.

Most people who have the goal to become an administrator get caught up in the day to day of their current position. If they teach, they get caught up in the day today of being a great teacher. If they are a counselor, they get caught up in the daily grind of being an awesome counselor.

They lose focus on small steps and strategies required to put them in position to get a greater opportunity. However, if you're touching base with your career influences, you're going to keep focus and more importantly, you're strengthening that relationship with people who matter.

When opportunities become available, they're going to pick up the phone and speak on your behalf.

Repetition equals reward in the end. Success is a numbers game. If you do the same thing repeatedly, you have no choice but to be successful.

Here is what you need to remember when interacting with your career influencers. If they suggest an article for you to read, read that article. Highlight it and make notes. Send your feedback to your career influencer.

If your career influencer suggests a book, read the book. The next time you communicate with them, reference a chapter in the book that you read. This gives them feedback and lets them know you value their suggestions.

If your career influencer recommends some type of professional development, sign up and complete the learning experience.

In other words, allow your career influencer to be a resource.

People really want to have an impact on the lives of others. I think we discussed that in section one.

If you allow these industry leaders to have an impact on your career, they will take stock in you. They will want you to be wildly successful, because if you're wildly successful, then they have bragging rights.

It's just like we do with kids. When they excel, you don't want any type of compensation. All you want to do is brag about it. You want to say that I worked with that kid, and he or she is now doing great things.

Your career influencers want the exact same thing.

Here is your 7th assignment.

Touch base with your five career influencers and set up the verbal agreement, the verbal agreement to communicate at least once per month. This can be done in person, on the telephone, or through a virtual meeting. Then add it to your calendar you created in section six.

Remember to be consistent and proactive when meeting with your five career influencers.

Action Items

- ✓ Make sure to sign up for our weekly newsletter at https://FutureAdministrators.com

- ✓ Attend one of our Future Admin Live events and consider joining our community at https://FutureAdministrators.com/live/

- ✓ Are there any challenges or obstacles you'll have to overcome in setting up your calendar? How are you going to handle it?

_____
_____
_____
_____
_____
_____

- ✓ What is one question you want to ask each career influencer in your next meeting?

_____
_____
_____
_____

SECTION EIGHT

Stand Out with Your Cover Letter, Resume, and References

Every school has what are called spirit weeks. During these days, the school has certain themes and opportunities to participate in something festive. For example, schools often have a tacky day, where staff, teachers, and students, wear colorful clothing that are mismatched and crazy looking. Another day may be centered on school pride where everyone wears a school t-shirt or school colors.

Recently, my school had a superhero day during our homecoming week. Students, faculty, and staff, wore Superman, Wonder Woman, Green Lantern, and Captain America costumes. To stand out, I took a different approach to this spirit day. I created my own superhero called Engagement Man. This newly created character's power was to engage all students in classrooms nationwide. I had a gold cape with a blue T-shirt decorated with a giant gold E.

Do you think I stood out? Of course, I did!

Everyone wanted to know, who is engagement man? How did you get that idea? Well, I want all my teachers to be more engaged.

Therefore, I created a superhero called engagement man.

I stood out and that makes the difference. Remember, it's key to stand out. You want to be different when it comes to others, who want to become school administrators.

It's very competitive. Remember, on my last administrative opening, more than 100 people applied for the position. What makes you the number one candidate?

Now let's get to where we're going with this lesson. You are going to need some tools when you start putting yourself out there.

This includes a cover letter, resume, and references.

5 Steps Cover Letter Formula

I'm going to give you a five-step formula to make your cover letter stand out. You can search Google and get all kinds of tips on the best cover letter, but I'm going to give you some tips that will make your cover letter a little different.

Look at the sample cover letter.

HARRY T. CLOVER, M.ED
77 Branchville Ct. • Charlotte, North Carolina 12345
(704) 123-4567 • harrytwizard@gmail.com

February 22, 2013

Dr. Whoever is in charge
Chief Human Resources Officer
School District
1234 School District Street
Charlotte, NC 12345

Dear Dr. Whoever is in charge,

During my senior year of high school, I decided to enter the field of education after taking Mrs. Sue Johnson's teacher cadet class. I was inspired by her passion for teaching and learned the foundation of what it takes to be a great educator. I also learned the importance of building relationships with students, parents, and other stakeholders.

Since then, I have had the opportunity to serve as a teacher, lead teacher, and program director.

I believe that our young people will change the world. It is our responsibility as professional educators to provide the education, support, and resources, in order for them to believe they can do it too.

My experiences below will make me an ideal candidate for a middle or high school administrator:

- I currently serve as **the instructional leader for Big Blue High School's Freshman Academy**, which includes 115 students, 9 teachers, and an administrative assistant.
- I am the **Blue Watch Lead Teacher**, a support program consisting of 14 team members (administrators, counselors, teachers, social worker, and a community liaison) to monitor academic assistance and interventions for identified students.
- I served as the **Instructional Leader and program director for Johnny Nelson's Freshmen Win**, a program consisting of a guidance counselor, literary coach, 10 teachers, and more than 250 students needing additional academic support and behavior management to successfully graduate.
- **I utilized a proactive approach to behavior management and gender based classes** to reduce freshmen discipline referrals in the Freshmen Win Program by 50%.

In addition to my experience above, I have a solid educational foundation and a passion for working with young people. I believe in having strong communication with all stake holders, working collaboratively with all team members, and cultivating a positive environment for students.

Thank you for your time and consideration.

Respectfully,

Harry T. Clover

Harry T. Clover

Step 1: Why did you choose education?

The first step in our five-step formula for cover letters is to explain why you chose education. Answer this question in about three to four sentences. While you are formulating your response, consider the following prompts:

Why are you excited about education?

Who inspired you to become an educator?

What do you want to accomplish in the field of education?

Here is how this question is answered in our sample cover letter.

"During my senior year of high school, I decided to enter the field of education. After taking Mrs. Sue Johnson's Teacher Cadet class, I was inspired by her passion for teaching and learned the foundation of what it takes to be a great educator. I also learned the importance of building relationships with students, parents, and other stakeholders."

In just a few sentences, the person explained how and why they chose education as a career.

Step 2: What positions have you held?

Write down all the positions you have served as an educator. Sum this up in about one to two sentences. You may have held the position of a teacher, counselor, or graduation coach.

Now here's a tip. You always want to refer to yourself as an instructional leader.

Here is how we addressed step 2 in our sample cover letter.

"Since then, I have had the opportunity to serve as a teacher, lead teacher, and program director."

As you can see, the person was able to describe three positions held in one sentence.

Step 3: Personal Statement!

If you have completed the assignment in section five, you already have your personal statement or 60 second commercial.

You should share your personal statement with everyone and including it in your cover letter is a great wat to do this.

Here is an example.

"I believe that our young people will change the world. It is our responsibility as professional educators to provide the education, support, and resources in order for them to believe they can do it too."

Does that personal statement sound familiar?

It's my very own personal statement. Every chance I get, I share it with those who are around me.

Step 4: List your experiences.

Step number four is to simply list all your experiences that will make you a qualified candidate for a job in educational administration. To make it easier for your reader to understand, use bulleted points.

Here is an example.

"My experiences below will make me an ideal candidate for a middle or high school administrator.

- *I currently serve as the instructional leader for Big Blue High Schools Freshman Academy, which includes 115 students, 9 teachers and an administrative assistant.*
- *I am the Blue Watch lead teacher, a support program consisting of 14 team members, administrators, counselors, teachers, a social worker, and a community liaison to monitor academic assistance and interventions for identified students.*
- *I serve as the instructional leader and program director for Johnny Nelson's Freshman Academy, a program consisting of a guidance counselor, literacy coach, 10 teachers, and more than 250 students needing additional academic support, and behavior management to successfully graduate.*
- *I utilized a proactive approach to behavior management and gender-based classes to reduce freshmen discipline referrals in the freshman program by 50%."*

I'm going to encourage you to review section twelve, the bonus lesson. You will learn a strategy that you can employ at your school and add to your cover letter and resume'.

Step 5: Conclusion

In your conclusion statement, you want to make sure you share that you are a believer in teamwork and collaboration.

Every administrative team is going to require teamwork and a strong work ethic. This is where you want to illustrate that you too believe in those things.

Here is an example.

"In addition to my experience above, I have a solid foundation and a passion for working with young people. I believe in having strong communication with all stakeholders, working collaboratively with all team members, and cultivating a positive environment for students. Thank you for your time and consideration respectfully."

In our example, the header includes the candidate's name, address, telephone number, and email address in a clear to read font.

It also has the name and address of the person the cover letter is being sent to.

That's the formula. If you utilize these suggestions when writing your cover letter, it's going to stand out among all the other cover letters.

Tips to Help Your Resume' Standout

A resume, also known as a curriculum vitae (CV), is a document that summarizes an individual's education, work experience, skills, and other relevant information. It is typically used as part of a job application to demonstrate the candidate's qualifications and suitability for a particular job or position.

A typical resume includes sections such as a personal summary or objective statement, education history, work experience (including job titles, dates of employment, and responsibilities), skills (both hard and soft), and any relevant achievements or certifications. The format and content of a resume may vary depending on the industry, job level, and specific job requirements.

A well-written resume should be concise, easy to read, and tailored to the specific job or industry being applied for. It should highlight the most important and relevant information and demonstrate the candidate's suitability for the job in question.

Here are 7 general tips for writing a great resume.

-Tailor your resume to the job: Customize your resume for each job you apply for by highlighting the most relevant qualifications, skills, and experiences. Review the job description carefully and match your resume to the job requirements.

-Keep it concise: Employers may receive hundreds of resumes for one job opening, so it's important to keep your resume concise and easy to read. Aim for one to two pages and use bullet points to highlight key information.

-Use strong action verbs: Begin each bullet point with a strong action verb to make your accomplishments stand out. Examples include "managed," "implemented," "created," and "improved."

-Quantify your achievements: Use numbers and data to demonstrate your accomplishments and impact. For example, instead of saying "improved test results," say "increased standardized test scores by 30%."

-Proofread and edit: Before submitting your resume, make sure to proofread it thoroughly and edit any errors. Ask a friend or mentor to review it as well and consider using a grammar checker tool to catch any mistakes you may have missed.

-Use a professional format and font: Choose a professional-looking font such as Arial, Calibri, or Times New Roman, and use a font size of at least 10-12 points. Use a consistent format throughout the resume, with clear headings and bullet points to make it easy to read.

-Include relevant keywords: Many employers use applicant tracking systems (ATS) to screen resumes before they are reviewed by a human. To increase your chances of passing the ATS, include relevant keywords from the job description throughout your resume. However, make sure not to overuse keywords or include irrelevant ones, as this may be seen as spamming and could harm your chances of being selected.

Look at our sample resume'!

HARRY T. CLOVER, M. ED

77 Branchville Ct. • Charlotte, North Carolina 12345
(704) 123-4567 • harrytwizard@gmail.com

EDUCATIONAL PROFILE

Results Oriented • Team Leader • Communicator
• Relationship Builder • Learner • Teacher

A proven educational leader with the ability to motivate others in a supportive and cooperative environment to reach and exceed expectations for the advancement of young people. Key accomplishments include:

- **Instructional Leader / Big Blue Program**, a program consisting of 40 students with academic and behavior challenges. Through mentoring, academic monitoring, and character education, grades have improved by 38%.
- **Managed the "No Zeroes" campaign for Big Blue High School**, which resulted in a 40% reduction in failure compared to the previous year.
- **Utilized a proactive approach to behavior management and gender-based classes** to reduce discipline referrals in Johnny Nelson High School's freshmen academy by 50%.

KEY SKILLS

• Team Building	• Detail Oriented	• Conflict & Dispute Resolution
• Critical Thinking Skills	• Leadership Development	• Professional Development
• Time & Behavior Management	• Public Speaking	• Teaching

PROFESSIONAL EXPERIENCE

Instructional Leader / Teacher
BIG BLUE HIGH SCHOOL – Charlotte, NC   2017 – Present

- **Instructional and Visionary Leader for the Big Blue Program**
- Developed and implemented a curriculum in accordance with school district guidelines.
- Assisted students with class work and adhered to scheduled daily lesson plans.
- Supervised student behavior and intervened as necessary.
- Tracked students' progress and provided individual feedback.
- Managed the "No Zeroes" campaign, an initiative where students committed to complete all assignments.

Instructional Leader / Teacher
JOHNNY NELSON HIGH SCHOOL – Columbia, SC   2016 – 2017

- **Instructional Leader for the Freshman Academy**, which includes 115 students, and 9 teachers, specializing in gender-based classes.
- Referred students to school counselors and other personnel when necessary.
- Developed assignments and prepared tests designed to gauge proficiency.
- Ensured that curriculum was centered around the abilities of each class.
- Provided assistance to students before during and after class as needed.
- Offered counseling to students in accordance with district guidelines.
- Prepared monthly progress reports and quarterly grades.
- Supervised student behavior and intervened as necessary.

EDUCATION AND AFFILIATIONS
Master of Educational Administration • Grand Mountain University – Fox, FL
Bachelor of Science in Biology Education • Charlotte University – Charlotte, NC

CERTIFICATIONS
Professional Teaching Certification and Biology and General Science • N.C. Certified Evaluator
• Secondary Principal Certification

PRESENTATIONS
"A Tale of Two Programs Thriving Together; AP and IB" • Presenter at Secondary Teachers – Nashville, TN
"Big Blue, a Support Program for Students" • Presenter at Closing the Achievement Gap – Charlotte, N.C.
Lead Teachers Panel • North Carolina State Department. – Charlotte, N.C.
"Incorporating Space Science in the Classroom" • Presenter at NSTA – Myrtle Beach, S.C.

TECHNICAL SKILLS
Knowledgeable and experienced with Windows XP, Vista and 7. Applications include Word, Excel, Outlook, PowerPoint, Access, Publisher, Project, HTML, Acrobat Reader, Novell GroupWise, and Internet Explorer, mobile devices, iPod/Podcasting, RSS, and Blogs. Adept with scanners, digital cameras, video cameras, and printers.

You can always use Google to find more general information about writing the best resume'.

However, the most important part of your resume' is the top portion.

Education Profile

Your educational profile is nothing more than four to seven buzz words that describe your strengths as an educator. Here is an example.

Results Oriented, Team Leader, Communicator, Relationship Builder, Learner, and Teacher.

Those are some great buzz words to describe a person who will be value added to an administrative team.

Your Body of Work Profile

Now the next section of our sample resume' is your body of work. This section describes key things you have accomplished in your educational career. You want to include percentages and key points describing your abilities.

Let's look at the example.

A proven educational leader with the ability to motivate others in a supportive and cooperative environment to reach and exceed expectations for the advancement of young people.

Key accomplishments include:

Instructional Leader in the Big Blue Program. A program consisting of 40 students with academic and behavior challenges. Through mentoring, academic monitoring, and character education, grades have improved by 38%.

Managed the "No Zeroes" campaign for Big Blue High School, which resulted in a 40% reduction in failure compared to the previous year.

Utilize a proactive approach to behavior management and gender-based classes to reduce discipline referrals in Johnny Nelson High School's Freshman Academy by 50%.

Again, that's the area where you show what you've done to assist and help improve the schools you're currently working or schools you have served in the past.

Key Skills

The next section of your resume includes key skills that you have in a bulleted easy to read format. Here is an example.

Team Building, Critical Thinking Skills, Time and behavior Management, Detail Oriented, Leadership Development, Public Speaking, Conflict and Dispute Resolution, Professional Development, Teaching.

In this section, you wanted to include skills that you possess, which make you an ideal candidate.

The rest of your resume is standard. You put the schools or places you've worked, the positions, and the times you worked there.

Concentrate on what's at the top of your resume' because decision makers will definitely look at that section.

Letters of Reference

Letters of reference, also known as letters of recommendation, are written statements provided by an individual who knows the job candidate and can vouch for their skills, abilities, and character. Letters of reference are typically used as part of a job application to provide additional evidence of the candidate's qualifications and suitability for a particular job or position.

Letters of reference may be written by supervisors, colleagues, teachers, or other professionals who have worked closely with the candidate and can attest to their skills and abilities. The letter should include specific examples of the candidate's work and accomplishments, as well as any relevant personal qualities, such as teamwork, leadership, or problem-solving skills.

When requesting a letter of reference, it's important to ask for permission and provide the letter writer with information about the job or position being applied for, as well as a copy of the candidate's resume and any other relevant information. It's also important to follow up with a thank-you note or email to express appreciation for the time and effort spent writing the letter.

Getting a strong letter of reference can be an important factor in securing a job. Here are some tips on how to obtain a letter of reference:

-Choose the right person: Select someone who can speak to your qualifications, work ethic, and character. This person should have a professional relationship with you and be familiar with your work. To get a job as a school administrator, make sure you get a reference from your principal or current supervisor, department chairperson, and a co-worker.

-Ask in advance: Give the person enough time to write the letter. Ask at least two weeks in advance and provide a deadline for when you need the letter.

-Provide the person with information about the job you are applying for, the skills required, and any relevant accomplishments or experiences that you would like them to highlight in the letter.

-Provide the person with a copy of your resume or CV, a list of your accomplishments, and any other relevant information that they may need to write the letter.

-Let the person know that you are available to answer any questions they may have or provide additional information.

-Follow up by sending a thank-you note to the person after they have written the letter. Also, follow up with the employer to ensure that they received the letter.

-Maintain a positive relationship: Stay in touch with the person who wrote the letter and keep them informed of your career progress. They may be a valuable resource in the future.

-Do not wait to the end of year to ask for a letter of reference (It's best to ask at the beginning of the year.)

-Share your resume' or an information sheet summarizing your accomplishments to help those writing your reference

Remember, the letter of reference reflects your character and qualifications, so it's important to choose someone who can write a strong and positive letter on your behalf.

Here is your 8th assignment.

Take time and develop the best cover letter that you can, organize your resume, as we discussed in this lesson, and think about who you want to give you letters of reference. Then, ask them for their support by writing you a letter.

Action Items

✓ Make sure to sign up for our weekly newsletter at https://FutureAdministrators.com

✓ Attend one of our Future Admin Live events and consider joining our community at https://FutureAdministrators.com/live/

✓ What experiences have you had will make you a great educational administrator?

_____

_____

_____

_____

✓ Who needs to give you a letter of reference?

Principal / Current Supervisor:

_____

Department Chairperson:

_____

Co-Worker:

_____

SECTION NINE

Strategies to Get Opportunities in School Administration

Before you employ the three strategies described in this section, you have to believe the following.

One: You deserve to be an educational administrator.

Two: You will do what's necessary to give you the advantage over the competition.

Three: You must employ strategies that you learn in this book.

Four: The number one way to get a job in school administration is to ask the right people.

Strategy #1: Ask your 5 career influencers and opportunity gatekeepers to give you opportunities they are aware of.

Ask your five career influencers and all your opportunity gatekeepers inform you of opportunities in administration. Remember, you should have a list with contact information of every opportunity gatekeeper you meet. Your five career influencers and opportunity gatekeepers are your hiring team.

Here is a template you can use for an email or phone conversation to ask for your next opportunity.

****

Hello _____,

As you know, my goal is to impact and service a greater number of young people. Are you aware of any opportunities in the coming year that may be suitable for me?

Please keep me in mind.

As always, let me know if I can be of assistance to you.

****

If you have built great relationships, you will get meaningful responses from your hiring team. This is the number one strategy to get the results you desire.

Here are a few things to remember:

-You need to be proactive. It's competitive, which means you need to do a combination of things to get yourself out there.

-Don't get stuck on one or two schools. You need to select several districts and schools to look at.

-You already have tips on a cover letter, resume, and letters of reference. It's important to utilize these tools to help you get an opportunity to serve.

Strategy #2: Send your three tools to the HR Director and principal of schools that have a position posted.

Our second strategy will involve the three tools (cover letter, resume, and letters of reference) described in section eight.

After identifying several schools and districts you would like to work in, send an email to the principals and human resources director attached with your three tools.

You also need to send a physical letter to the HR director and the principal. Remember, most people are not going to do this. They're going to simply apply and wait.

In your email and physical letter, you use the wording in our template:

****

Subject: Consideration for Assistant Principal Position

Hello (HR Director or Principal),

I have attached a cover letter, resume, and three letters of reference.

Please consider me for an interview for the position of Assistant Principal and instructional leader.

Thank You,

Your Name

123-123-1234

****

Make sure you include your cover letter, resume, and letters of reference as an attachment.

In addition to the email, don't forget to send physical mail including your 3 tools.

If you want to be ultra-aggressive, send your information out to several different districts whether the job is posted or not.

Remember, your objective is to get yourself out there. It's possible to get opportunities. Monitor district websites regularly and look for postings. If you do that, doors will begin to open, and you'll realize the possibilities.

Strategy #3: Strategically use traditional methods.

The third strategy is your traditional means of applying for the jobs. It means simply applying online.

Look at the districts and schools you want to work in and apply online. You may have to apply for administrative pools, where districts are collecting applications from educators interested in school leadership. Typically, they pull candidates from these pools to interview.

There's one advantage to applying online.

It doesn't matter how you get an opportunity to move further in the hiring process, you will be required to fill out an application online. If you already have it completed, that will be one less thing you'll have to worry about.

Here is your 9th assignment.

Decide on the districts and schools you want to work in and start contacting principals and HR directors through e-mail and physical mail.

Make sure you make a list and track all the places you apply.

Also, continue to monitor district websites and take action when you notice available openings in school administration.

Action Items

- ✓ Make sure to sign up for our weekly newsletter at https://FutureAdministrators.com

- ✓ Attend one of our Future Admin Live events and consider joining our community at https://FutureAdministrators.com/live/

- ✓ Make a list of schools and districts you want to work in.

_____
_____
_____
_____
_____
_____
_____
_____
_____

- ✓ Are you willing to relocate to a new area? _____

- ✓ How far are you willing to commute each day? _____ miles

SECTION TEN

How to Have a Great Interview

In this section, we will give you tips and strategies to have a great interview. However, if you follow the steps outlined in this resource, you will already have the job before sitting down at the interview table.

In other words, the interview would be a formality and a part of the process. Either way, you want to do your very best. You don't want a poor interview, which could work against you.

Having a great job interview can increase your chances of landing your next opportunity.

Use these general tips to help you prepare for and excel in a job interview:

Study the district of the school where you're having your interview.

What are the demographics of that district? What are the goals of the district? Are there any special initiatives?

If the district has an initiative where all students are expected to test on a 7th grade reading level, you can communicate that when you're sitting at the interview table. That will give you the slight edge to know the initiatives.

Who is the superintendent?

Does he or she have a favorite quote or book? If you knew that information, you could share it during an interview session.

The only way you're going to get these specific details is through research.

You can start by using Google, which will give you a wealth of information. You also need to review the district and school websites. Remember, this is about giving yourself every advantage over other candidates.

Study the school you are applying to work in.

What does the typical student look like at the school? Are there any school goals? For example, it may be a school goal to have more rigor in the classroom. If you know this, you can give your ideas on incorporating rigor into the classroom and what rigor looks like for you.

How can you be a benefit and help the school accomplish a particular goal? Are there any special programs at the school?

For example, it may be a school with a magnet program, specializing in engineering. How can your skillset align with supporting an engineering magnet?

What are the test scores? Are kids at that school suffering or scoring lower in math? Do they need additional interventions?

As an educational leader, how can you support that goal of helping young people in that math area? What can you do to be an asset?

Who was the principal of the school? What if you knew that the principal's favorite book was, *"Who Stole my cheese?"*

You could literally talk about the book in an interview? That's going to impress the principal.

Practice common interview questions: Review common interview questions and practice your responses in advance. This will help you feel more comfortable and confident during the interview.

Dress appropriately: Dress professionally and appropriately for the company's culture. It's better to be overdressed than underdressed.

Arrive early: Arrive at least 10-15 minutes early to allow time to find parking, check in with receptionist, and get settled.

Make a good first impression: Be friendly, polite, and professional when you first meet your interviewer. Offer a firm handshake, maintain eye contact, and smile. <u>Don't forget to interject your 60 second commercial or personal statement.</u>

Listen carefully: Listen carefully to the questions being asked and make sure you understand what the interviewer is looking for in their responses.

Be specific: When answering questions, be specific and use examples from your past experiences to demonstrate your skills and abilities.

Ask questions: Ask thoughtful questions about the company, the position, and the company culture. This shows that you're interested and engaged.

Follow up: Send a thank-you note or email to your interviewer within 24 hours of the interview. This is a great opportunity to express your gratitude and reiterate your interest in the position.

Remember, the key to a great interview is preparation and practice. By taking the time to research the district and school, practice your responses, and make a great first impression, you'll be well on your way to securing the job you want.

Here is your 10th assignment.

Do your research of schools and districts that you are interested in. Put this information in a three-ring binder for you to study, which will better prepare you for an interview.

Use the school information sheet to help track your research.

Continue monitoring district websites for opportunities and contacting your five career influencers.

How To Get a Job In School Administration

FUTURE ADMINISTRATORS

School Information Sheet

Name of School: _____

Principal: _____ Number of Students: _____

Demographics: _____

School Mascot: _____

Mission Statement:
_____
_____
_____

Special Programs:

1. _____

2. _____

3. _____

Recent Accomplishments:

1. _____

2. _____

3. _____

Test Scores:
_____
_____

Graduation Rate: _____

Additional Information:
_____
_____
_____

Copyright 2020 FutureAdministrators.com

Action Items

✓ Make sure to sign up for our weekly newsletter at https://FutureAdministrators.com

✓ Attend one of our Future Admin Live events and consider joining our community at https://FutureAdministrators.com/live/

✓ How confident are you with answering questions during an interview?

_____
_____
_____

✓ What areas do you need to work on to perform your best on an interview?

_____
_____
_____

✓ Are there any other resources you have available to help you have a great interview?

_____
_____
_____

SECTION ELEVEN

Popular Assistant Principal Interview Questions

In section 11, we're going to review popular assistant principal questions and answers. In addition to this resource, you need to create a database of assistant principal questions and answers.

Review and practice answering them on a consistent basis. This will help you gain confidence, which will result in having a great discussion about opportunities in school administration.

Now, let's get started with a few questions and great answers to consider.

Why do you want a career in education as an administrator?

Great Answer: As an educational leader in the classroom, I have valued building relationships with students and teaching them to think and perform on a higher level. As I've had the fortune of observing great administrators, who have made a difference on a school level, I would like the opportunity to share ideas, employ successful strategies, work with stakeholders, and collaborate on a school level for positive change.

In your opinion, what are the characteristics of an effective team?

Great Answer: An effective team allows all members to have a true voice, where input and sharing ideas is expected and encouraged. All members of the team trust each other and understand their roles and responsibilities. Each member has skills that are complimentary to others on the team and the goals and missions of the organization are realized.

Collaboration is a common place and healthy debate which creates great initiatives that are employed to improve academic achievement.

What is your philosophy on discipline and how do you handle behavior issues?

Great Answer: I believe we must support students and engage them on expectations for success in the classroom. This includes behavior and sharing strategies for difficult situations. While discipline should not be punitive, after prior interventions have failed, students may need time to think about their actions.

Teachers must have an environment that is conducive to learning. As a school leader, we must support those efforts.

How do you handle a tough situation with a parent?

Great Answer: It's important to give the facts of the situation, allow parents to respond, and listen. Listening is key.

Share the school's expectations with the parents and present interventions that will be put in place as the result of an action. Communicate with parents that you are supportive and their child will get past the current situation.

Follow up with the parent after the initial conversation to show support and answer any possible questions.

How would you handle a situation with a teacher who is not performing up to expectations?

Great Answer: It's important to support teachers and provide resources and professional development for success. First, you must share with the underperforming teacher what is expected. Next, present the facts of what you observed. Allow the teacher to respond and share their reasoning. Finally, present interventions for improvement.

This may include participating in a virtual training, trying different teaching strategies, or complying with a specific action. Develop a plan for improvement and monitoring by making additional observations or a follow up meeting.

How do you make sure all students are experiencing success?

Great Answer: It's critical that school leaders consistently monitor, review data, and make changes if needed to create a culture where academic achievement is the norm. This requires reviewing test results, sharing with teachers, students, and parents. Through collaboration, create initiatives for change and follow through.

It's also important to get constant feedback from parents, teachers, and students to get their ideas for improvement and consider those responses in decision making.

Where do you see yourself in five years?

Great Answer: I hope to use my talents and experiences to move this school forward. I hope to have learned from this administrative team and be ready for other opportunities if it's right for me. I believe in focusing and doing my very best in my current position, and my goal is to have a greater positive impact on young people.

Share an example of how you have had an impact on academic achievement throughout the entire school.

Note: This is where you would benefit from reviewing our bonus lesson.

Great Answer: As the director of Big Blue, an academic assistance program, I worked with underperforming students at my current school. Through monitoring their progress, creating academic plans for each student, communicating with teachers, and parents, student grades improved by 40%.

This helped our school to realize their goal of reducing overall student failure.

How would you help teachers monitor classroom management?

Great Answer: It's important for teachers to understand they are supported when it comes to an environment that encourages learning. This includes having a classroom free from disruptions because of behavior. As an administrator, it's important to encourage teachers to share names of students who present potential problems after they have made initial parental contact. When I get these names, I will follow-up to have a conversation with the student and parent.

When behavior concerns are reported to my office, I will handle each case with the classroom environment in mind and share expectations with the student and parents.

I will also follow up to make sure the issue or problem is resolved.

How would you help build a positive school culture?

Great Answer: Positive school culture involves encouraging an environment where communication is important. Everyone sees through a different lens and sharing helps the organization improve culture. Success should be rewarded. Incentives should be used to help with engagement. The entire team needs opportunities to collaborate and reflect on current performance.

Decisions should be made after getting valuable input from the team and everyone should be updated regarding data and issues pertaining to the school.

What are your strengths and weaknesses?

Note: This is a personal question, which requires you to communicate your own thoughts.

Great Answer: I can look at the big picture, evaluate what needs to be done, and delegate to members of my team to acquire the desired result. My communication skills are a positive, and I have the ability to build positive relationships with people on all levels.

I tend to work very hard at times and forget to rest and allow myself to rejuvenate. That's because I'm passionate about impacting young people.

However, I am aware of working too much and believe in practicing self-care when needed.

How would you encourage teacher leadership at our school?

Great Answer: Teachers must understand their role is valuable to the success of the school. The teacher is the most important variable in the classroom.

As an administrator, it's important to create opportunities for teachers to lead. This requires delegating tasks and initiatives for teachers to lead. For example, a teacher can be asked to manage an after-school tutoring program. A teacher could be assigned to lead an academic promotion at a school for English or math. If administrators are intentional about teacher leadership, teachers will respond favorably.

How would you handle a conflict between a teacher and student?

Great Answer: As an administrator, I know it's important to have a classroom culture where academic achievement is the standard. To handle such a conflict, I will speak with the student and the teacher separately, to get both sides.

I understand the teacher is not always right, and if that is the case, the teacher and I will work out a solution to the problem.

When speaking with the student, I will discuss possible solutions to the issue, and review better ways the situation could have been handled if needed.

I will talk with the parents, discuss the situation, and allow them to voice their concerns. Finally, I will review our plan to successfully move forward.

How would you improve parent participation at our school?

To positively engage parents in their child's education, it's important to have several strategies in place to encourage involvement. First, there needs to be a strong commitment from teachers to contact parents on a regular basis regarding student progress. This includes emailing, calling, sending letters, and requesting parent conferences. Parents need to be aware of positive things their young people are accomplishing as well as areas where improvement is needed. Parent communication would be monitored and emphasized on a regular basis during regular faculty meetings.

Next, there needs to be opportunities during the year where parents can come to open houses and special programs to see what their children are doing at school. To increase attendance at such programs, it's important to personally invite parents to events and involve their children in activities. This may require making phone calls and sending out announcements.

Thirdly, parents need to be personally asked to serve on school committees. It's important for them to understand why their support is needed, especially when it comes to making school decisions and launching new initiatives.

There needs to be several forms of communication with parents, which should include a regular parent electronic newsletter, school web page, school Facebook page, school Twitter page, and videos showcasing events and happenings of the school. To get the message out for more parent involvement, it's important for the school to have a presence where parents communicate.

Finally, parents need to understand that there is an open-door policy for them to make inquiries, discuss problems, and make suggestions for improvement. If parents feel good about school leadership and its vision, they will participate with the right strategies in place.

How should teachers measure student performance?

Great Answer: It's important for teachers to focus on summative and formative assessments and use that data to adjust instructional strategies. Teachers need to focus on developing common tests, quizzes, and activities, which will allow much needed information for discussion in Professional Learning Communities.

In addition to tests and quizzes, teachers need to consistently check for understanding throughout the daily lesson. This includes strategies such as exit slips, discussions, graphic organizers, short presentations, individual white boards, and think-pair-share.

I am also a strong believer in teachers taking ownership of outcomes and student performance.

How would you increase community involvement in our school?

Great Answer: For a school to be successful, it is important to involve all stakeholders. This requires providing and creating opportunities for community organizations to forge partnerships.

As an assistant principal, I would develop a board of community and business partners that meets on a regular basis. This will give organizations and community leaders an opportunity to share ideas, suggestions, and support the school financially.

I would also plan a community fair at the school to give parents and students an opportunity to learn what services are available in the local area.

I would have a community awards program to celebrate and show appreciation for community involvement. This would encourage and retain participation from stakeholders.

What do you consider the core business of public education, and why?

In my opinion, the core business of public education is developing citizens that are able to successfully compete and contribute in a global arena through teaching and learning. Creative thinkers and leaders are in high demand. It is the obligation of public educators to provide resources and skills students need to be sufficient productive members of society.

What do you believe distinguishes a good teacher from a great teacher?

Good teachers can effectively teach and transfer knowledge to students they can use to be successful. In addition to doing things that are characteristic of good teachers, great teachers are able to build strong relationships, develop positive character traits, leadership skills, and create memorable moments that students will ultimately transfer to others while successfully competing in a changing world.

How would you incorporate technology into the structure of our school to facilitate active student engagement.

During a lesson, teachers should have 3 – 5 transitions to keep students engaged. I would encourage teachers to incorporate the use of technology in at least one of those transitions. This would get teachers using technology on a consistent basis.

I would also schedule appropriate professional development to help teachers learn strategies and ideas to incorporate the use of technology in their curriculum. It's critical for teachers to understand what good technology integration looks like in a classroom. Students can use technology to create projects, enhance presentations, strengthen academic skills through online assessments, and obtain information from web-based resources to better understand concepts.

In addition to professional development, I would ask teachers to meet in professional learning communities to share ideas, resources, and strategies to successfully use technology to engage students.

What are the characteristics of an engaging unit of study?

An engaging unit of study should include an outline and specific objectives students are required to master. This outline should include strategies that activate prior knowledge and allow for activities to build and expand current knowledge.

An engaging unit of study should also include goals and learning targets for students.

There should be 5 – 10 activities where students are able to use technology, collaborate, and formulate an idea based on concepts taught.

Engaging units of study should have a culminating activity to summarize the unit and give students the opportunity to present or create a final product utilizing objectives previously discussed.

How do you ensure diversity in a school setting?

Diversity builds strength in a high school setting, which is why it is important to consider stakeholders from various backgrounds when making decisions or employing school wide initiatives. As the school leader, it is important to intentionally reach out to parents and teachers of all races and socioeconomic statuses as well as leadership organizations such as the Parent Teacher Student Organization (PTSO), School Improvement Council (SIC), and booster clubs to encourage them to become investors in making our school successful. This will require setting up meetings with individuals to express how valuable their participation is to the victory of their school and community. Ownership of new strategies occurs when everyone is invited to give input and a sense that each constituency has a voice in ensuring the success of our school.

Diversity in student leadership should also be considered in school-based programs, assemblies, and organizations. Participation from students with different backgrounds and cultures will enhance the school climate and make it a dynamic place for learning.

Do you stay abreast of current research and reading? Summarize a concept that you read lately and explain how you plan to use this information.

Note: This is a personal question, which requires you to communicate your own thoughts.

Great Answer: In the book, *The Principal* by Michael Fullan, a new philosophy of school leadership is described. It is not enough for the principal to be the direct instructional leader of his or her school. Success depends on the principal's ability to be the "lead learner" and build professional capacity among the school's faculty. Ultimately, this means the principal must be less of a micro-manager and more of a balanced leader that has the ability to motivate people to do even more.

It's critical to give people skills by investing in their growth as educators. When this happens, people are more accountable, which often results in expected progress. Principals should focus on providing professional development to build leaders and allow them to lead by using student data to make improvements in instruction in order to get better academic achievement.

Questions you may want to ask at the end of your interview.

What qualities are you looking for in an assistant principal?

What do you expect of me in the first six months?

Can you tell me what a typical day might look like?

What do you enjoy about working at this school?

What are the priority areas for improvement in the next school year?

In general, how well do parents engage with the school?

What are some challenges you expect the assistant principal to face in the next twelve months?

How will success be measured?

How would you describe the leadership style of the principal?

Can you tell me more about how students interact with the teachers?

Here are some additional tips to help you answer interview questions effectively:

Listen carefully: Listen carefully to the question and make sure you understand what the interviewer is asking before you respond. If you're unsure, ask for clarification.

Be concise: Keep your answers concise and to the point. Avoid rambling or going off on tangents. Aim to answer the question within 1-2 minutes.

Be specific: Use specific examples from your past experiences to demonstrate your skills and abilities. This helps to make your answers more concrete and memorable.

Highlight your strengths: When asked about your strengths, be prepared to provide specific examples of how you've demonstrated those strengths in the past. This shows the interviewer that you have a track record of success.

Address your weaknesses: When asked about your weaknesses, be honest but also show that you're working to improve. Discuss a specific weakness and what you're doing to overcome it.

Stay positive: Maintain a positive attitude throughout the interview, even if you're asked challenging questions. Avoid speaking negatively about previous employers or experiences.

Remember, the key to answering interview questions effectively is to be prepared, specific, and concise. By using specific examples from your past experiences and maintaining a positive attitude, you'll make a great impression on your interviewer.

Here is your 11th assignment.

Build your database of interview questions and practice daily!

Action Items

- ✓ Make sure to sign up for our weekly newsletter at https://FutureAdministrators.com

- ✓ Attend one of our Future Admin Live events and consider joining our community at https://FutureAdministrators.com/live/

- ✓ When will you practice answering interview questions on a regular basis?

  _____
  _____
  _____

- ✓ List three people who can help you practice answering interview questions.

  _____
  _____
  _____

- ✓ Where else can you find sample interview questions and answers?

  _____
  _____
  _____

SECTION TWELVE

How to Start an Academic Assistance Program

One of the biggest problems candidates have when looking for an opportunity in school administration is lack of experience. As a classroom teacher or counselor, it is challenging to take on administrative duties that will help you get an edge during an interview.

Decision makers want to know what you have done outside the four walls of a classroom to impact student achievement.

How have you made an impact on the entire school and what administrative duties have you been able to complete?

There is one thing you can do which will check off most of the boxes required when it comes to getting administrative experience.

You can start an Academic Assistance Program!

An Academic Assistance Program is more in depth than a tutoring program. It's a program that requires monitoring students, employing multiple interventions, communicating with parents, and collaboratively with administrators.

It's a great way to show your leadership outside the classroom and how you have impacted academic achievement on a school level.

Steps to Starting an Academic Assistance Program

Step 1: Volunteer your services by asking your principal if you can set up an academic assistance program for a selected number of students. (It's best not to go beyond 40 students unless you have a team of other staff members to assist you.)

Most principals will agree to your proposal. You may have to show more specific details, which is where our resources come in handy.

Step 2: Decide on a name. This will require speaking with co-workers and students to get ideas. It's great to collaborate with a team, because these individuals may end up helping you with your initiative.

When you are at the interview table, you can mention that you serve as the director of the named program. That's administrative experience.

Step 3: Have a meeting with school leadership to come up with a selection process and determine criteria for the students you will work with. This may include students who are failing subject areas.

Step 4: Set a date to have all student recommendations to your new academic assistance program.

Step 5: Send out an invitation letter to parents of students who were recommended. Your letter should include a start date for the program.

Step 6: Meet with each student and parent individually to discuss and develop an Individual Success Plan (ISP). You may want to get other teachers to help you with this task, which is great to help with your ability to build a team and delegate responsibilities. These meetings can be in person or virtually.

Step 7: Start meeting with your students on a weekly basis to discuss progress, character education, get student feedback, and promote incentives.

Step 8: Track progress of all your students and communicate with parents. This will require working with teachers, parents, and administrators.

Note: It's important to track the data. You can look at the percentage of your students who have improved academically. Attendance and behavior are also great data points to look at and record to show the success of your program.

Take a look at a template for an Academic Assistance Program.

The "Choose a Name" Program

An Academic Assistance Program Designed

for Student Improvement

Program Overview:

A program aimed at helping identified students successfully improve academically through mentorship, academic support, and partnerships with stakeholders.

Key Program Components:

Dedicated Teacher Leader

A dedicated teacher leader is assigned to the "Choose A Name" Academic Assistance program and is responsible for monitoring student performance, planning special programs, incentives, and making connections with students.

Individualized Success Plan

Every student in the "Choose a Name" Academic Assistance program has an individualized success plan to help them accomplish established goals.

Mentoring

 Students will meet on a regular basis, either virtually, or in a group setting to learn from volunteer speakers. During these sessions, career options, character development, and personal growth strategies will be discussed.

Incentive Program

Students will be rewarded each week with incentives from local businesses such as free food coupons.

Student Meetings

Students will meet our teacher leader to review individual success plans and strategies for improvement. Parents will be invited to participate in these meetings.

Partnership with Parents

Parents will receive a quarterly report on the progress of our programs and opportunities to participate in initiatives. This includes help with planning, establishing community partnerships, and assisting with program events.

How Are Students Selected

Students are recommended by teachers and administrators. Parents may also recommend their student if they feel it will be a benefit.

Program Goals

-   Academic Improvement
-   Individual Success Plan for Each Student

- Student Mentoring
- Parental Involvement

The School Leadership Team

Mr. John Doe, Principal

Ms. Sussie Que, Assistant Principal

Mr. Mickey Mouse, Assistant Principal

Teacher Leader

Your Name, Program Director

Let's Review the Forms

You can use the following forms to help track data and assist with managing your program.

<u>Academic Assistance Program Template</u>

The first form we're going to discuss is the Academic Assistance Program template. It includes all the key program components and a little blurb about each one. Make it your own.

<u>ISP (Individual Success Plan)</u>

It includes information on the student's grade level, lead teacher, test scores, and an area to include specific strategies for improvement.

Teacher Observations

If you are interviewing students and setting up an ISP, you may talk to their current teachers, and learn some things about that student to include in your plan of action.

Plan of Action

Your plan of action may include weekly tutoring, a homework focus plan, and a self-assessment plan.

Parent Communication Section

This section is an area to record conversations with parents regarding the student's progress.

Self-Progress Assessment Form

This form is designed for the student to take responsibility for his or her own actions. They have to look at their current grades, attendance, and behavior.

It also requires the student to write down strategies for improvement.

Homework Focus Plan Form

This form is designed to help students organize and complete their homework on a consistent basis. They have to list assignments, record time spent on homework, and whether or not they understood the work.

The Tutoring Help Form

This form is designed to help a student recognize area they need assistance in. They have to write down questions and their level of understanding. There is also a section for parent and teacher communication.

Hopefully, you see the benefits of setting up and directing your very own academic assistance program. In addition to having a greater impact on student learning, you will gain valuable experiences managing the program.

Here's your 12th assignment!

Review the forms you can use in your academic assistance program. Take a look at the steps to getting started and begin taking action. Come up with your program's name. Set up a meeting with your principal to discuss volunteering to manage such a program. Who knows? There may be some funding where you can actually get paid. See if you can establish a team of co-workers, teachers, and instructional assistants who can help you build your program.

Start the program.

Homework Focus Plan

Directions: Complete a section for every homework assignment given to you by your teacher.

Date	Subject	Assignment

Time Started: _____   Time Finished: _____   Total Time: _____

☐ I understood and completed the assignment   ☐ I have questions and need additional assistance   Write down your questions in the space provided below

1>_____

2>_____

3>_____

Date	Subject	Assignment

Time Started: _____   Time Finished: _____   Total Time: _____

☐ I understood and completed the assignment   ☐ I have questions and need additional assistance   Write down your questions in the space provided below

1>_____

2>_____

3>_____

Created by Vondre' T. Whaley 7/28/16

Individual Success Plan

Student:	Date:
Grade Level:	Lead Teacher:

Background Information

504	Please Circle One Yes No (If Yes, attach to this document)
IEP	Please Circle One Yes No (If Yes, attach to this document)
Resource	Please Circle One Yes No
Self-Contained	Please Circle One Yes No

Testing Information

Type of Test	
Time of Year	
Type of Test	
Time of year	

Teacher Observations :

_____
_____
_____
_____

Plan of Action for Improved Performance

☐ Weekly Tutoring   ☐ Home Work Focus Plan   ☐ Self - Assessment Plan

_____
_____
_____
_____
_____
_____
_____
_____

Individual Success Plan

Parent Communications

Name: _____ Phone: _____

Email: _____ Address: _____

Date	Please Circle One	Details
	Email - Telephone Conference	
	Email - Telephone Conference	
	Email - Telephone Conference	
	Email - Telephone Conference	
	Email - Telephone Conference	
	Email - Telephone Conference	
	Email - Telephone Conference	
	Email - Telephone Conference	
	Email - Telephone Conference	
	Email - Telephone Conference	
	Email - Telephone Conference	
	Email - Telephone Conference	
	Email - Telephone Conference	

Name: _____ Period: _____ Date: _____

Tutoring Help Form

Directions: Write down the questions or problems you're having in class and get your parent's signature. Bring this form with you to tutoring so we can measure your progress.

Questions:

1. _____
_____

2. _____
_____

3. _____
_____

Parent Signature: _____ Date: _____

Date Of Session: _____ Time Started: _____ Finished: _____

Please check one regarding the questions above.

1. __ I Now understand   __ I'm still having problems and need further help.

2. __ I Now understand   __ I'm still having problems and need further help.

3. __ I Now understand   __ I'm still having problems and need further help.

Student Signature: _____ Date: _____

Teacher Comments:

Teacher Signature: _____ Date: _____

Created by Vondre' T. Whaley 7/28/17

SELF PROGRESS ASSESSMENT FORM

Date: ___/___/___   Student: _____   Mentor: _____

Classes (Use Power school to fill out the information below.)

_____	Grade: _____	Absences: _____
_____	Grade: _____	Absences: _____
_____	Grade: _____	Absences: _____
_____	Grade: _____	Absences: _____
_____	Grade: _____	Absences: _____
_____	Grade: _____	Absences: _____
_____	Grade: _____	Absences: _____
_____	Grade: _____	Absences: _____

Issues That Need Work:
(Is there anything keeping you from being successful? Is there something that needs to be addressed?)

_____
_____
_____
_____
_____
_____

Note: Absences are directly related to student achievement. Students who attend school regularly have higher grades compared to students with attendance issues.

What Actions Steps Do I Need To Take To Improve?

1. _____
2. _____
3. _____
4. _____
5. _____
6. _____
7. _____

Student's Signature: _____   Date: ___/___/___

Mentor Recommendations   ☐ Other: _____

☐ Admin. Conference   ☐ Guidance Conference   ☐ Attend teacher tutoring sessions   ☐ Parent Teacher Conference   ☐ Attendance Team

Created by V.T. Whaley 8/2/20

Action Items

- ✓ Make sure to sign up for our weekly newsletter at https://FutureAdministrators.com

- ✓ Attend one of our Future Admin Live events and consider joining our community at https://FutureAdministrators.com/live/

- ✓ What's the name of your academic assistance program?

_____
_____
_____

- ✓ List three people who can help you manage your program.

_____
_____
_____

- ✓ What is the start date for your program?

_____
_____
_____

Top Tips for Educators Looking to Get a Job In School Administration

Obtain the necessary qualifications.

Most school administrator positions require at least a master's degree in education or a related field. Additionally, obtaining a certification or licensure in educational administration can increase your chances of getting hired.

Gain relevant experience.

In order to become a school administrator, it is important to have relevant experience as an educator. Consider taking on leadership roles within your current school or district, such as serving on committees, mentoring new teachers, or coordinating school-wide initiatives.

Network with other educators.

Attend professional development conferences and events, join professional organizations, and connect with other educators in your field. Building relationships with other administrators can help you learn about job openings and gain referrals.

Develop strong communication skills.

School administrators must be able to communicate effectively with students, parents, teachers, and other stakeholders. Work on developing strong communication skills, both written and verbal.

Keep up to date with education trends and policies.

Stay informed about changes in education policy and trends in teaching and learning. This knowledge can be helpful in interviews and when discussing educational initiatives with stakeholders.

Be prepared for the interview process.

Research the school district and the position you are applying for. Practice answering interview questions and be prepared to discuss your experience and leadership philosophy. It can also be helpful to prepare a portfolio showcasing your work as an educator.

By following these tips, educators can increase their chances of landing a job as a school administrator.

Top Tips on Building Strong Relationships with Decision Makers

Research the school district and decision-makers.

Learn as much as you can about the school district and the decision-makers who will be involved in the hiring process. Look for information about their backgrounds, values, and priorities.

Attend school board meetings.

Attend school board meetings to learn more about the district's priorities and to get to know the decision-makers. This can also be an opportunity to ask questions and offer your input on issues affecting the district.

Connect with decision-makers on social media.

Follow decision-makers on social media and engage with their posts. This can help you build a relationship with them and show that you are interested in their work.

Volunteer in the district.

Volunteer in the district to show your commitment to the community and to get to know decision-makers. This could involve serving on a committee or helping with a school event.

Request an informational interview.

If possible, request an informational interview with a decision-maker. This can be an opportunity to learn more about the district and to ask questions about the hiring process.

Stay in touch.

After the interview process is over, make sure to stay in touch with decision-makers. This could involve sending a thank-you note or reaching out to offer your assistance with any initiatives or projects.

By building strong relationships with decision-makers, educators can increase their chances of getting hired as school administrators. Remember to be genuine, respectful, and persistent in your efforts to connect with these individuals.

Top Tips on Gaining Experience Outside the Classroom

Serve on committees.

Many schools and districts have committees that focus on various aspects of school administration, such as curriculum development, school safety, or student support services. Serving on a committee can provide teachers with valuable experience working collaboratively with other educators to make decisions and implement initiatives.

Take on leadership roles.

Teachers can also take on leadership roles within their schools or districts. This might involve serving as a department head, mentoring new teachers, or coordinating school-wide initiatives.

Participate in professional development.

Professional development opportunities can provide teachers with new knowledge and skills related to school administration. Teachers might consider attending workshops or conferences focused on leadership, educational policy, or other relevant topics.

Volunteer in the community.

Volunteering in the community can also provide teachers with administrative experience. For example, teachers might volunteer with local youth organizations or serve on a nonprofit board of directors.

<u>Pursue advanced degrees.</u>

Pursuing an advanced degree in educational administration or a related field can provide teachers with in-depth knowledge of school leadership and management.

By gaining administrative experience outside the classroom, teachers can broaden their skill set and increase their chances of advancing in their careers. It can also help them develop a more comprehensive understanding of the challenges and opportunities involved in school administration.

In conclusion, we have outlined several of the top tips to securing an opportunity in school administration.

Hopefully, you realize the blueprint outline in this book will give you an extreme advantage if implemented on a consistent basis.

The ball is in your court. You deserve to be a school administrator. All you need to do is believe your dream to serve can become a reality. Get started today by building your network with the right people who can help you help even more students.

Resources

Future Administrators

A weekly newsletter designed to give tips and strategies to help educators get opportunities in school administration.

https://FutureAdministrators.com

Templates and Resources

You can get all the templates and resources mentioned in this book at https://FtureAdministrators.com/templates

Are you looking for professional development (in person or virtual)?

Contact Vondre T. Whaley

vondre@gmail.com

https://twitter.com/VondreWhaley

https://VondreWhaley.com

If you are interested in professional development, writing books, and developing courses, consider joining our professional network of educational consultants at https://IntentionalEducators.net

Made in United States
Troutdale, OR
02/08/2025